Wrap Yo...

An Affirmation Book... ...eels Like a
Warm Hug (Daily Gifts of Happiness and Self-Love)

Victoria Davis

DJTS
PUBLISHING

Table of Contents

Improve Your Life with Affirmations

 ear reader,

Welcome to this book of positive affirmations for women. In today's world, it can be easy to get caught up in the hustle and bustle and lose sight of our own worth and value. That's why it's so important to take time for ourselves, to focus on our own self-care and self-love, and to remind ourselves of the incredible individuals that we are.

This book is designed to do just that. Each page is packed with powerful affirmation that will help you to cultivate a deeper sense of love and acceptance for yourself. As you read through these affirmations, take a moment to pause, reflect, and let the words sink in. Allow yourself to truly believe in the power of these affirmations and the impact they can have on your life.

Remember, you are worthy of love and care, and it's never too late to start building a more loving relationship with yourself. So, take a deep breath, let go of any doubts or fears, and let these affirmations guide you on your journey to self-love and self-acceptance.

With love and positivity,

Victoria

Affirmations 1-365

1) I am joyful.

2) I am wise.

3) I am loved.

4) I am safe.

5) All is well.

6) I am strong.

7) I love life.

8) I am a lady.

9) I am appreciated.

10) I am capable.

11) Life is easy.

12) I'm so lucky.

13) Life is safe.

14) I am valuable.

15) I am worth it.

16) I can do this.

17) I am abundant.

18) It's all good.

19) I am graceful.

20) I love myself.

21) I am beautiful.

22) I deserve love.

23) I trust myself.

24) Life is for me.

25) Today is my day.

26) I love being me.

27) I am so blessed.

28) I am significant.

29) Today is my day.

30) I am always safe.

31) My head is clear.

32) Life is so great.

33) Life supports me.

34) Women are strong.

35) Being me is okay.

36) Life is very easy.

37) I love having fun.

38) I deserve success.

39) I can do anything.

40) This is a new day.

41) I am a manifestor.

42) It's good to be me.

43) I am true to myself

44) Life is on my side.

45) Life is good today.

46) Today is a new day.

47) I enjoy letting go.

48) I am free to be me.

49) I let life live me.

50) I believe in myself.

51) I am light and free.

52) This is a great day.

53) Life rewards action.

54) Women are beautiful.

55) Women are so strong.

56) My body is a temple.

57) Life is so much fun.

58) I am easy to please.

59) Women are wonderful.

60) Life loves me today.

61) My life is a miracle.

62) I always have plenty.

63) I accept my good now.

64) I love being a woman.

65) Women are so amazing.

66) I make the rules now.

67) I'm fun to be around.

68) I am proud of myself.

69) What a wonderful day.

70) Life starts right now.

71) I manage my time well.

72) We are all one family.

73) Life is truly amazing.

74) Everyone is my friend.

75) I am a powerful woman.

76) Abundance feels great.

77) Life loves me so much.

78) I look and feel great.

79) What a wonderful life.

80) I am my own authority.

81) Every woman is a star.

82) I have all that I need.

83) I am a creative genius.

84) I trust my inner voice.

85) I am inherently worthy.

86) I deserve to feel good.

87) I am proud of who I am.

88) Women are so beautiful.

89) Whatever I want, I get.

90) My growth is unlimited.

91) Practice makes progress.

92) All my dreams come true.

93) Life loves me right now.

94) I see my future clearly.

95) I love myself endlessly.

96) Today is an amazing day.

97) My life is a gift to me.

98) I'm proud to be a woman.

99) I am excited about life.

100) I am safe wherever I go.

101) Life is easy and simple.

102) I am protected and safe.

103) Life is truly a miracle.

104) My smile is captivating.

105) I am enough just as I am.

106) I can be anything I want.

107) My heart is open to love.

108) My body is ready for fun.

109) Forgiveness sets me free.

110) All that I do is blessed.

111) Living my dream life now.

112) Good things happen to me.

113) My life is full of magic.

114) This is my time to shine.

115) I choose peace right now.

116) I feel so good right now.

117) My success is inevitable.

118) I am enough, just as I am.

119) I am brave and courageous.

120) It's okay to ask for help.

121) All is well with my world.

122) Today is my new beginning.

123) I am loveable and lovable.

124) Love flows through me now.

125) Life is always on my side.

126) It is safe for me to soar.

127) I am a magnet for success.

128) I deserve all good things.

129) Life is taking care of me.

130) I inspire others to dream.

131) My potential is limitless.

132) Women are powerful beings.

133) I am at peace with myself.

134) I am so amazingly blessed.

135) I am confident and capable.

136) I am enough just as I am.

137) I am the light of my world.

138) I am loved, no matter what.

139) All my dreams are possible.

140) I am the master of my life.

141) My past does not define me.

142) Today is an incredible day.

143) Life loves me, and so do I.

144) I love who I am right now.

145) Life supports me right now.

146) Abundance is my birthright.

147) It's always an amazing day.

148) I love myself for who I am.

149) I am at peace with what is.

150) I'm doing everything right.

151) My needs are being met now.

152) My life is wonderful today.

153) Life is so very good to me.

154) Abundance is all around me.

155) I am feminine in every way.

156) I am a fun, playful person.

157) My kids are safe and happy.

158) As a woman, I'm so awesome.

159) My body is healthy and fit.

160) I am a woman of competence.

161) Life loves me; I love life.

162) I am valuable and important.

163) I am a diamond in the rough.

164) Each day is a new beginning.

165) Life is so fun and exciting.

166) I am very beautiful as I am.

167) It's okay to make mistakes.

168) The world is friendly today.

169) I am an instrument of peace.

170) I feel peace surrounding me.

171) I am a magnet for abundance.

172) I am doing everything right.

173) I'm beautiful in my own way.

174) I let go, and I am at peace.

175) There's enough for everyone.

176) I am at peace with the past.

177) My life is in perfect order.

178) I am living my dreams today.

179) Life supports me completely.

180) Everything works out for me.

181) Women are amazing beings.

182) Everything always works out.

183) I am worthy of great things.

184) I deserve to be happy today.

185) I create beauty in my world.

186) I have so much love to give.

187) Today, I am radiantly happy.

188) I love myself more each day.

189) I am capable beyond measure.

190) What I feel is okay to feel.

191) I am a woman of great worth.

192) I am a good and loyal friend.

193) Everything is going to be ok.

194) Every day is a new beginning.

195) Self-love fills me up inside.

196) Life is on my side right now.

197) Life loves me beyond measure.

198) I'm ready for anything today.

199) Being positive feels so good.

200) Only good comes to me always.

201) I am loved and cared for now.

202) There is plenty for everyone.

203) I am women celebrating women.

204) I choose happiness right now.

205) Tomorrow will be even better.

206) I have a winning personality.

207) My heart is light and joyful.

208) I feel so safe and protected.

209) My beliefs become my reality.

210) My brain is relaxed and calm.

211) My mind is focused and clear.

212) I feel like a child of nature.

213) I am beautiful inside and out.

214) I am trusting and trustworthy.

215) All of my dreams are possible.

216) My body is healthy and strong.

217) I love myself unconditionally.

218) I let people live their lives.

219) What joy fills my heart today.

220) I am a blessing to this world.

221) My mind is focused on success.

222) I deserve happiness right now.

223) I am winning the game of life.

224) I am happy, healthy, and free.

225) I feel calm and serene inside.

226) I am always peaceful and calm.

227) Life supports me in every way.

228) I have everything that I want.

229) Life is on my side completely.

230) My body is the perfect weight.

231) I am a strong confident woman.

232) I have a strong, capable body.

233) Life is fun, easy, and simple.

234) My body is strong and healthy.

235) My creativity inspires others.

236) I am worth it, and so are you.

237) As I am now, so will I become.

238) Today will be a wonderful day.

239) I am beautiful, inside and out.

240) I am full of joy and happiness.

241) I have a lot of inner strength.

242) My emotions are valid and real.

243) I am grateful for this new day.

244) All people are inherently good.

245) Money flows to me effortlessly.

246) Today, I am ready for anything.

247) Each new day is a fresh start.

248) I see life through loving eyes.

249) The best comes out of me today.

250) I love who I have become today.

251) I deserve all the good in life.

252) I am a magnet for good fortune.

253) I am filled with joy and light.

254) Life is now working out for me.

255) Life is beautiful, and so am I.

256) What a day this is going to be.

257) I am safe and loved, right now.

258) I am the master of my own life.

259) My body is healthy and vibrant.

260) It's easy for me to feel great.

261) It's okay for women to be loud.

262) I love having relationships in my life.

263) Love flows easily into my life.

264) People respect me just as I am.

265) I'm in full control of my life.

266) Life loves me, and I love life.

267) Life is working out for me now.

268) I am perfect just the way I am.

269) It feels so good to be a woman.

270) I am a caring and giving woman.

271) I am a radiantly healthy woman.

272) I am worthy of love and respect.

273) I have a lot to offer the world.

274) Today is a good day to be alive.

275) Today, I will make myself proud.

276) I can feel the magic in my life.

277) I am unique in all of the world.

278) Everything works out for me now.

279) Calmness floods my entire being.

280) My future is brighter than ever.

281) My mind is set on success today.

282) I am a great and powerful woman.

283) Perfect health is my birthright.

284) I am my reason for feeling good.

285) This is the best day of my life.

286) I trust my intuition completely.

287) Women are radiant and beautiful.

288) I am a self-fulfilling prophecy.

289) I love the person I have become.

290) My life is full of love and joy.

291) My life is full of joy and ease.

292) I am a powerful, creative being.

293) I am blessed in every way today.

294) My future is bright and hopeful.

295) My greatness will not be denied.

296) I am a happy and grateful woman.

297) I am always growing and learning.

298) I am deeply loved by many people.

299) Life works out for me every time.

300) My future is bright and exciting.

301) I'm becoming more self-confident.

302) Abundance comes easily to me now.

303) I release all guilt from my life.

304) My words carry great power today.

305) Thanks to everyone I know, today.

306) My day is messy, and that's okay.

307) It is safe for me to be here now.

308) All of my dreams are coming true.

309) Every day gets better and better.

310) Life is safe for me, and so am I.

311) Life is always taking care of me.

312) Healthy relationships nurture me.

313) I am free to make my own choices.

314) Everything is working out for me.

315) Today, I create my own happiness.

316) Life loves and supports me fully.

317) My goals are all coming true now.

318) I deserve to feel good right now.

319) I always get exactly what I want.

320) I have an amazing sense of style.

321) I have an amazing sense of humor.

322) My body has a natural glow to it.

323) Life loves me, and I love myself.

324) I'm safe, and everything is okay.

325) I do what works for me right now.

326) I am willing to learn new things.

327) Just for today, I will not worry.

328) Every day of my life gets better.

329) I have the strength to carry on.

330) Things are starting to go my way.

331) Life is beautiful and full of joy.

332) I am limitless and have no limits.

333) My past mistakes do not define me.

334) Today already counts as a success.

335) I am smart, confident and capable.

336) I am blessed with an amazing life.

337) Today I am open to receiving love.

338) I am one with the energy of money.

339) I love the person that I am today.

340) All of my desires are coming true.

341) My body is healthy, slim and trim.

342) I love and approve of myself 100%.

343) My heart overflows with joy today.

344) Everything works out for me today.

345) I forgive myself, unconditionally.

346) I want the best life has to offer.

347) I am going to be successful today.

348) My life is in perfect order today.

349) All that I desire comes to me now.

350) Today is a great day because . . .

351) All my dreams manifest, with ease.

352) My body is beautiful in every way.

353) My family love me unconditionally.

354) People appreciate me just as I am.

355) My mind is always sharp and clear.

356) Life is fun. I enjoy every moment.

357) I have a positive outlook on life.

358) I am loved and supported by others.

359) I have nothing to hide from others.

360) I am whole and capable of anything.

361) I am surrounded by positive people.

362) Today's a great day to start fresh.

363) I have the power to change my life.

364) Today, things will work out for me.

365) My intuition is stronger than ever.

Affirmations 366-730

366) I expect to have a great day today.

367) I allow myself to succeed in life.

368) I am the creator of my own destiny.

369) I love the person that I am today.

370) I have a beautiful and happy home.

371) My needs are met before they arise.

372) Life is a party, and I am the host.

373) Life supports me right this moment.

374) I deserve to be rich and happy now.

375) I forgive myself and others, today.

376) All of life's wounds can be healed.

377) Everything happens for my own good.

378) Each day I am growing and learning.

379) I am so grateful to be alive today.

380) I am the creator of my own reality.

381) Today is my day; it's all about me.

382) All is well in my world, right now.

383) I am loved and cared for right now.

384) I have the strength to do anything.

385) Today, I am filled with enthusiasm.

386) My intuition is my strongest guide.

387) I love and approve of myself fully.

388) I'm calm and at peace with my body.

389) I radiate pure joy and inner peace.

390) Life is unfolding perfectly for me.

391) People accept me the way that I am.

392) My life is a beautiful masterpiece.

393) My mind is flexible and discerning.

394) Whatever happens, I will handle it.

395) I am a bright star in the universe.

396) I was born with creative abilities.

397) I feel happy, healthy and balanced.

398) I will not be held back by my past.

399) I am a woman with power and wisdom.

400) I am a woman of peace and serenity.

401) Every day is another chance at life.

402) I am in control of my own happiness.

403) I am limitless and I have no limits.

404) I open my mind to new possibilities.

405) I am a money magnet. Money loves me.

406) My mind is clear, calm, and focused.

407) Today, I am free to be my true self.

408) I release all need to punish myself.

409) It is OK to give myself what I need.

410) My body is healthy and strong today.

411) I release all guilt about yesterday.

412) Every day is a new beginning for me.

413) Today is full of joy and prosperity.

414) Things are getting better every day.

415) I am joy, I am love, and I am light.

416) The world is beautiful, and so am I.

417) I love life, and life loves me back.

418) I am living the life that I deserve.

419) I am an unstoppable force of nature.

420) Life is taking care of me perfectly.

421) Life has been very, very good to me.

422) It's always the right time for _____.

423) I am strong, confident and powerful.

424) I deserve the absolute best in life.

425) I love and accept myself completely.

426) I am safe to trust my intuition now.

427) It's easy for me to feel good today.

428) My hormones are completely balanced.

429) I have the best figure in the world.

430) My eyes are bright and full of life.

431) Life supports me in everything I do.

432) I easily manifest all of my desires.

433) Abundance flows freely into my life.

434) I always know the right thing to do.

435) I deeply and completely love myself.

436) I am in tune with my hormonal cycle.

437) In every adversity lies opportunity.

438) My mind is clear and calm right now.

439) I trust myself. I know my own worth.

440) My body is perfect exactly as it is.

441) Nature blesses me each and every day.

442) I am lovable and accepting of others.

443) I am powerful, capable and confident.

444) I am a kind and compassionate person.

445) Life is a journey, not a destination.

446) Life is full of beauty and adventure.

447) I am a magnet for love and happiness.

448) Problems are only temporary setbacks.

449) Life is meant to be fun and exciting.

450) I love myself just as I am right now.

451) I give myself permission to be happy.

452) I have a beautiful and happy family.

453) I approve of myself, wholeheartedly.

454) All of my dreams are coming true now.

455) I let go of all anger and resentment.

456) I am living in the moment, right now.

457) I only attract the best into my life.

458) I take time out for myself every day.

459) Life is working out for me right now.

460) All is well in every area of my life.

461) I am surrounded by the power of love.

462) Today, I focus on being my best self.

463) I am a magnet for love and abundance.

464) I am at peace with what is right now.

465) I have all the love I need right now.

466) I attract loving people into my life.

467) Everything is working out in my life.

468) I am overflowing with love and light.

469) I am blessed with wisdom and insight.

470) I am strong, powerful and incredible.

471) I deserve to be surrounded by beauty.

472) It's okay for women to take up space.

473) It's okay for me to show my emotions.

474) Women are beautiful just as they are.

475) Love surrounds me in every way today.

476) The future looks radiantly beautiful.

477) I am content with who I am right now.

478) My life is full of peace and harmony.

479) Life is working out perfectly for me.

480) My creativity is thriving, right now.

481) I feel so grateful to be alive today.

482) I deserve to pamper myself every day.

483) I am proactive, I make things happen.

484) As a woman, I am capable of anything.

485) I take care of everything in my life.

486) When it's meant to be, it's up to me.

487) I am kind and compassionate to others.

488) Today, I choose to live in the moment.

489) I love and accept myself just as I am.

490) I can manifest anything that I desire.

491) I deserve love, success and happiness.

492) Life is full of beauty and excitement.

493) I am enjoying my journey through life.

494) Life is very easy, just the way it is.

495) I am kind to my mind, body, and soul.

496) Today is going to be a wonderful day.

497) I am always doing the best that I can.

498) I am safe and secure in a loving world

499) I release all fear and anxiety, today.

500) The love I seek comes to me naturally.

501) My mind is free from worry and stress.

502) Everything works out for me right now.

503) I trust what life has in store for me.

504) Every day is a new opportunity for me.

505) I am always guided by my inner wisdom.

506) I love myself and everything about me.

507) My heart is open to all possibilities.

508) Loving myself is as easy as breathing.

509) I am cheerful, fun, and full of light.

510) I trust that the Universe has my back.

511) The Universe loves me unconditionally.

512) Every day brings new gifts to my door.

513) I radiate happy feelings all day long.

514) The more fun I have, the happier I am.

515) I listen to the wisdom deep within me.

516) People respond to me in positive ways.

517) I choose to be happy and grateful now.

518) I believe in myself and all that I am.

519) My mind is calm, peaceful and focused.

520) I am powerful and capable of anything.

521) My heart beats with pure love and joy.

522) My creative talents are in full bloom.

523) My inner beauty radiates to the world.

524) I see myself and all others with love.

525) I love my life no matter what unfolds.

526) My soulmate is on their way to me now.

527) I celebrate all that makes me a woman.

528) As a woman I define beauty for myself.

529) I am making my body stronger every day.

530) My body is a powerful force of nature.

531) The only opinion that matters is mine.

532) I am healthy in body, mind and spirit.

533) I am a woman and I love being a woman.

534) My home is filled with light and love.

535) I love and accept myself for who I am.

536) I deserve to be happy and this is why.

537) My life is full of love, joy and peace.

538) I am a loving and compassionate person.

539) My thoughts are filled with positivity.

540) Everything always works out in the end.

541) I am making all of my dreams come true.

542) I am worthy of all good things in life.

543) I attract positive people into my life.

544) This moment is exactly as it should be.

545) Everything I need is already within me.

546) All my needs are met before I even ask.

547) Life has so much to offer me right now.

548) I am a beautiful and magnificent being.

549) Every day is filled with peace and joy.

550) I am powerful, positive, and motivated.

551) Success follows me wherever I go today.

552) Life is always working out for my good.

553) My heart is open; I am free; I am love.

554) I always do my best, and that's enough.

555) Life loves me; this is my home forever.

556) I accept myself for who I am right now.

557) It's safe for me to be alive right now.

558) Life is taking care of me in every way.

559) I release all tension and struggle now.

560) Today and all day, I am light and free.

561) The universe is conspiring in my favor.

562) Women support and build other women up.

563) I am naturally confident and care-free.

564) I see beauty everywhere in this moment.

565) My mind is free from worry and concern.

566) It's safe for me to express myself now.

567) Abundance flows into my experience now.

568) I am beautiful in mind, body, and soul.

569) Life supports me in every way possible.

570) It's easy for me to relax and have fun.

571) I easily find new ways to enjoy myself.

572) I let go of wanting to be someone else.

573) The most powerful thing I can be is me.

574) What I plant now, I will harvest later.

575) All of my cells are healthy and strong.

576) I will live to see my dreams come true.

577) Today I am free to make my own choices.

578) I have the strength to follow my heart.

579) I am a woman of excellence and success.

580) I am a positive and enthusiastic woman.

581) My skin is smooth, healthy and glowing.

582) I am confident, capable and dependable.

583) My worth has been established by nature.

584) I can handle whatever life throws at me.

585) I value and respect myself and my needs.

586) I can do anything that I set my mind to.

587) I am a survivor and nothing can stop me.

588) I am successful in everything that I do.

589) Life is full of love, joy and happiness.

590) Life is always working out for the best.

591) I think before judging others or myself.

592) I deserve to be happy, joyous, and free.

593) I release regret from my mind and heart.

594) I am a radiant being of light and love.

595) My words carry power and strength today.

596) My life keeps getting better and better.

597) My body is healthy, strong, and capable.

598) I make decisions easily and confidently.

599) I have everything that I need right now.

600) My day is filled with peace and harmony.

601) Today is an opportunity for me to shine.

602) I love my life just the way it is today.

603) The more I give out, the more I receive.

604) I love myself exactly as I am right now.

605) Every cell in my body vibrates pure joy.

606) Everything is good in my life right now.

607) I free myself of all pain and suffering.

608) People in my life respect me completely.

609) Today and every day, I choose happiness.

610) Women are amazing, beautiful and strong.

611) All of my needs are being met right now.

612) My heart is constantly filled with love.

613) It's safe for me to release my past now.

614) It's easy for me to stay positive today.

615) I am full of ideas and creative visions.

616) My mind is clear, focused, and powerful.

617) My life is filled with joy and laughter.

618) I am a radiant being of light and power.

619) I feel so blessed and supported by life.

620) I am getting more and more fit each day.

621) I am the only one in control of my life.

622) Today, I will release all my resistance.

623) I shall be successful in all that I do.

624) My life is one of endless possibilities.

625) I am a woman who is radiant with beauty.

626) I am a peaceful, calm and patient woman.

627) My body is healthy, strong and flexible.

628) The best times of my life are right now.

629) Each new day is a chance for me to shine.

630) I am beautiful and loving inside and out.

631) When one door closes, another door opens.

632) My mind is clear and focused on my goals.

633) Things always work out for me in the end.

634) I deserve to be happy and free right now.

635) I am an inspiration to myself and others.

636) I fly free like the beautiful butterfly.

637) My mind is filled with positive thoughts.

638) I am a major force for good in the world.

639) I am a magnet for good things in my life.

640) I am more than what happened in the past.

641) It's all working out for my highest good.

642) Everything in my life is going perfectly.

643) I am a work in progress, and that's okay.

644) People are inherently good, just like me.

645) I am healthy, happy, and whole right now.

646) I attract supportive people into my life.

647) Love rushes through me in all directions.

648) I feel the love in every cell of my body.

649) My life is filled with happiness and joy.

650) My body is healing itself on every level.

651) Life loves me and supports me completely.

652) As life happens to me, so I happen to it.

653) I am so happy and grateful now that . . .

654) Life is taking care of me amazingly well.

655) I am loved and supported unconditionally.

656) I have a clear vision of where I'm going.

657) People are always there when I need help.

658) As a woman, I am beautiful and fantastic.

659) I am self-confident, strong and powerful.

660) I am a source of positivity in the world.

661) My intuition never steers me wrong, ever.

662) Women deserve all the good in this world.

663) Women have the power to change the world.

664) I love and accept myself exactly as I am.

665) I have great willpower and determination.

666) My life overflows with happiness and joy.

667) I unconditionally love and accept myself.

668) I am focused, determined, and persistent.

669) I easily handle whatever I need to today.

670) Life always has the best in store for me.

671) Women's beauty is in their natural shape.

672) As I focus on the good in life, it grows.

673) I love who I am and how my life is today.

674) I wake up feeling ready to seize the day.

675) Today, I will focus on love and kindness.

676) I am beautiful because I accept who I am.

677) I deserve everything that is good for me.

678) I am a happy, relaxed and positive woman.

679) I am a smart, capable and talented woman.

680) I am able to cope with difficult emotions.

681) I am trustworthy; people can depend on me.

682) I am capable of anything I set my mind to.

683) Positive thoughts create positive results.

684) My life is full of joy, peace and harmony.

685) The Universe supports me in all that I do.

686) The path ahead of me is bright and cheery.

687) I am a radiant being of light and energy.

688) Life is good to me every day in every way.

689) I am at peace with myself and life itself.

690) I am in the right place at the right time.

691) My day is filled with peace, love and joy.

692) My mind is calm and peaceful at all times.

693) I allow myself to be who I am meant to be.

694) The more positivity in my day, the better.

695) My life is full of love and happiness now.

696) Today, I focus on what is good in my life.

697) Up, up, and away. That's where I go today.

698) I am free to be myself, just the way I am.

699) I am loved, supported, forgiven, and safe.

700) I am already happy, successful, and whole.

701) Every day, I'm making my dreams come true.

702) I am safe, protected, and loved right now.

703) My heart expands with gratitude every day.

704) My mind is clear and focused effortlessly.

705) I love myself completely, exactly as I am.

706) Every part of my life is filled with love.

707) The world is a better place because of me.

708) I am the best version of myself when . . .

709) Today, I choose to feel good about myself.

710) All of my desires are being fulfilled now.

711) I love it when people are attracted to me.

712) Women are beautiful just the way they are.

713) Everything in my world has perfect timing.

714) My life is just getting better and better.

715) The universe provides for all of my needs.

716) Everything in my life is positive and fun.

717) I am grateful for all the love in my life.

718) Each moment is filled with awe and wonder.

719) My body heals itself easily and perfectly.

720) All I need is already within me right now.

721) My presence helps others relax and let go.

722) The natural shape of my body is beautiful.

723) With every challenge comes an opportunity.

724) I choose to be enthusiastic about my life.

725) As a woman, I am both smart and beautiful.

726) I focus on the beauty of my face and body.

727) All people are beautiful in their own way.

728) It's okay to take up space on this planet.

729) I focus on the positive things in my life.

730) Anything is possible if I work hard for it.

Affirmations 731 - 1094

731) I am worthy of love, respect and happiness.

732) My happiness grows more and more every day.

733) Everything is working out for me right now.

734) My life is filled with peace and abundance.

735) A new romance will come into my life today.

736) I am a magnet for love, money, and success.

737) Life is gently taking care of me right now.

738) Every day is better than the one before it.

739) I am aware of my magnificence at all times.

740) It's all working out in my favor right now.

741) I am worthy of all the good things in life.

742) This very moment is the best one of my day.

743) My lifestyle is healthy, happy, and secure.

744) All of my hopes and dreams are coming true.

745) My life is full of exciting new adventures.

746) Each day in my life gets better and better.

747) Life loves me unconditionally, and so do I.

748) Life is taking care of me now, and so am I.

749) I trust that life is taking care of me now.

750) Healthy people come into my life every day.

751) The more I give, the more comes back to me.

752) My life has become blissful thanks to . . .

753) I have everything that it takes to succeed.

754) I follow my heart; it always leads me home.

755) Today I am making lots of progress at work.

756) All women deserve respect and appreciation.

757) Today, I simply relax in life's perfection.

758) Today, I create a wonderful day for myself.

759) I love to do the things that really matter.

760) Today, I give thanks for my many blessings.

761) I am filled with happiness, peace, and joy.

762) This world is a better place because of me.

763) Each day of my life gets better and better.

764) I approach life with wonder and excitement.

765) I am connected to all of life through love.

766) I attract abundance into my life every day.

767) Abundance flows into every area of my life.

768) All the love I need is within me right now.

769) I am a woman and I feel great about myself.

770) I am letting go of guilt, shame and regret.

771) I am letting go of fear and worry for good.

772) I am creative, resourceful and intelligent.

773) My home fills with peace, love and harmony.

774) My relationships are healthy and nurturing.

775) Life supports me in every way at all times.

776) No goal is too big for me to achieve today.

777) My life is filled with ease and perfection.

778) My life is filled with love and friendship.

779) My body is graceful and fluid when I dance.

780) I am a woman of excellence and distinction.

781) I love myself unconditionally, just as I am.

782) I accept myself for who I am, flaws and all.

783) My heart beats strong and healthy every day.

784) I am in control of my attitude and thoughts.

785) I am doing my best, and that is good enough.

786) I always attract loving people into my life.

787) All my relationships are healthy and loving.

788) I am completely safe from harm in every way.

789) I am grateful for the life I have right now.

790) My work is deeply satisfying and fulfilling.

791) I love and approve of myself wholeheartedly.

792) My life is full of love and happiness today.

793) I attract loving relationships into my life.

794) I am 100% responsible for my feelings today.

795) There is so much more for me to receive now.

796) My life is full of peace, happiness and joy.

797) My life is full of happiness and prosperity.

798) Today is the greatest day of my entire life.

799) Fear is only an illusion. It cannot stop me.

800) Creative ideas flow through me all day long.

801) I deserve all of the happiness in the world.

802) Every day in my life gets easier and easier.

803) My inner child feels loved and nurtured now.

804) I'm safe; the world is safe. We're all okay.

805) Every day of my life gets better and better.

806) I am one with life; all is well in my world.

807) All of my desires are coming true right now.

808) Life gives me exactly what I need right now.

809) The more time passes; the better things get.

810) Today, my life is getting better and better.

811) Life gives me all that I need and much more.

812) The more I lighten up, the better life gets.

813) My body is healing, regenerating and strong.

814) My life is unfolding perfectly in every way.

815) I am safe to express all of my feelings now.

816) My intuition is always guiding me perfectly.

817) Other women are healthy, happy and peaceful.

818) My mind is teeming with wonderful new ideas.

819) My mind is filled with positive power today.

820) I am safe and secure in all that I do today.

821) When life gets difficult, I face it head-on.

822) I radiate joy and success with every breath.

823) Abundance and prosperity are mine right now.

824) My inner beauty radiates out into the world.

825) I always have time to relax and be peaceful.

826) Great things are happening in my life today.

827) My body is my home, beautiful and well kept.

828) I look for opportunities in every challenge.

829) I choose to be a powerful and strong person.

830) My mind is clear, focused, calm and relaxed.

831) Life is exciting, fun and full of adventure.

832) As a woman, I am a masterpiece of evolution.

833) I excel in all that I set out to accomplish.

834) I am beautiful in every way, inside and out.

835) I love unconditionally and without judgement.

836) I can achieve anything that I set my mind to.

837) I am surrounded by an amazing support system.

838) I am a good friend, and others appreciate me.

839) Today is a new day, and I choose to be happy.

840) I am going to make my dreams come true today.

841) I am surrounded by an aura of love and light.

842) There is always something to be grateful for.

843) I have all that I need to be happy right now.

844) All things are possible to those who believe.

845) Every part of my life is improving every day.

846) I am radiant with health and happiness today.

847) This is the day that I have been waiting for.

848) I am full of positive energy and enthusiasm.

849) My work is deeply satisfying and fulfilling.

850) I can achieve anything that I put my mind to.

851) I see myself as smart, capable and resilient.

852) I allow myself to feel what I need to, today.

853) It's easy for me to let go of old habits now.

854) I am grateful and happy to be here right now.

855) Today, I let go of all my worries and doubts.

856) Wherever I go today good things happen to me.

857) Everyone's light is a blessing to this world.

858) All is well in my world; all is well with me.

859) I am abundant in all areas of life right now.

860) I release all limitations; only love remains.

861) I give out joy and receive it back in return.

862) I give out love, and it comes back in droves.

863) Everything happens at exactly the right time.

864) I give thanks that life is taking care of me.

865) What I focus on, I create more of in my life.

866) Today and every day, I am surrounded by love.

867) My life is filled with endless possibilities.

868) Every experience in my life serves a purpose.

869) As a woman, I am intelligent and full of joy.

870) I have everything that I need in this moment.

871) I have a healthy body that is full of energy.

872) I am an inspiration to everyone who knows me.

873) I am safe to express myself in every way now.

874) I am so grateful for all the good in my life.

875) I love the way women take care of each other.

876) I open myself up to receive love from others.

877) The Universe provides for me in amazing ways.

878) Every day of my life is better than the last.

879) Today, I allow joy to touch me deeply within.

880) I am surrounded by opportunities for success.

881) I love the process of getting to know people.

882) Every day, I feel better than the day before.

883) I have an amazing ability to succeed in life.

884) My happiness increases with every rising sun.

885) I deserve the very best in my life right now.

886) The best version of me is emerging right now.

887) I accept myself completely just the way I am.

888) My life is filled with peace and tranquility.

889) My thinking is accurate, relevant and useful.

890) I am surrounded by loving friends and family.

891) As a woman, I have the power to create life.

892) The universe flawlessly orchestrates my life.

893) I am a woman of honor, integrity and respect.

894) It is up to me whether I am happy or unhappy.

895) Life loves me; I love life; it's that simple.

896) I am confident in who I am and what I can do.

897) My opinions are valid and important to others.

898) I have inner strength and can handle anything.

899) It's okay to make mistakes; no one is perfect.

900) My life has a purpose, and I embrace it fully.

901) I have what it takes to deal with tough times.

902) Today, I will choose to be happy and positive.

903) I am surrounded by an aura of positive energy.

904) I can achieve anything if I believe in myself.

905) My life is full of joy, prosperity and health.

906) I deserve all the good that life has to offer.

907) I appreciate the gifts that life has given me.

908) Every day, I experience miracles in many ways.

909) I am becoming more and more relaxed every day.

910) My life unfolds perfectly for my highest good.

911) Blessings are everywhere in my life right now.

912) I am a magnet for joy, wealth, and prosperity.

913) My inner child feels safe and loved right now.

914) The more loving I am, the more love I receive.

915) My life is filled with joy, love and laughter.

916) I am optimistic about all that lies before me.

917) The world is a better place because I'm in it.

918) Life loves me and supports me unconditionally.

919) My body is healthy, strong and full of energy.

920) All women are naturally beautiful and radiant.

921) I am a source of love for all those around me.

922) All natural, organic foods make me feel great.

923) My body is the perfect weight and size for me.

924) I am a treasure trove of creativity and ideas.

925) Abundance flows easily into my experience now.

926) My heart overflows with positive energy today.

927) I am deeply fulfilled in all areas of my life.

928) I am surrounded by beauty, love, and laughter.

929) My life overflows with miracles and blessings.

930) Everything works out for me, I n every moment.

931) I am safe, secure, and protected at all times.

932) My mind is always open to positive new things.

933) Women are truly beautiful from the inside out.

934) My body has an amazing ability to heal itself.

935) Today, the only person who is in my way is me.

936) I deserve the love of a compassionate partner.

937) I am becoming more creative with each new day.

938) I am worthy to receive abundance in all forms.

939) Abundance flows towards me quickly and easily.

940) I choose to live my life without limits today.

941) My life is full of happiness, success and joy.

942) I am a woman who is willing to learn and grow.

943) Everything in my world is going so well today.

944) I am so incredibly happy for no reason at all.

945) I am kind, caring, and compassionate to others.

946) I am a divine, radiant being of love and light.

947) Life is always working out for my highest good.

948) Money flows to me through many different means.

949) I trust the flow of life to unfold in my favor.

950) My future is bright with endless possibilities.

951) I have all that I need to be successful today.

952) I am worthy of the best that life has to offer.

953) Life is working out for everyone all around me.

954) I get to enjoy success and happiness every day.

955) I am willing to let go of the past and move on.

956) Every day, I am becoming more and more relaxed.

957) I am safe and whole in the eye of the universe.

958) My past has made me the person that I am today.

959) I deserve the very best that life has to offer.

960) I deeply and completely love and accept myself.

961) Today, I am blessed with endless opportunities.

962) Every day, I get closer to achieving my dreams.

963) I'm grateful for everything that happens today.

964) I see beauty and love everywhere in this world.

965) Life has an abundance of gifts in store for me.

966) The Golden Age of peace is already here for me.

967) It is safe to feel good about myself right now.

968) Life is working out perfectly for me right now.

969) My life is filled with peace, love and harmony.

970) The energy of love fills every cell in my body.

971) The universe loves me so much more than I know.

972) I am a wonderful example to everyone around me.

973) Life works out perfectly for everyone involved.

974) All of the changes in my life are for the best.

975) Being a woman is the best feeling in the world.

976) Every day in every way I get better and better.

977) Today, I move through life with grace and ease.

978) My body is attractive and symmetrical in shape.

979) The harder that I work, the luckier that I get.

980) I attract all of the right people into my life.

981) All of life is working out for my highest good.

982) My thoughts are powerful and create my reality.

983) Each day, newer and better thoughts come to me.

984) Every new moment brings me closer to my dreams.

985) My body tells a story of the life I have lived.

986) I am willing to see how truly magnificent I am.

987) Every day I make progress no matter how little.

988) My life is full of things to feel grateful for.

989) It's okay if life doesn't go according to plan.

990) Great ideas come to me easily and effortlessly.

991) I will not be broken by the challenges of life.

992) My body feels healthy, nourished and energized.

993) I am open to new opportunities and experiences.

994) Life can be beautiful if I choose to make it so.

995) My life is full of abundance, joy and happiness.

996) I am surrounded by positive energy at all times.

997) I can create anything that I want to in my life.

998) All my relationships are healthy and supportive.

999) Money flows into my life in many different ways.

1000) My mind is filled with positive thoughts today.

1001) I give thanks for the many blessings in my life.

1002) I have everything that I need in life right now.

1003) Every day in every way, I get better and better.

1004) Everything always works out for my highest good.

1005) I am surrounded by peace and serenity right now.

1006) Creative ideas are flowing through me right now.

1007) Everything that happens is for my ultimate good.

1008) Nothing and no one can take away my inner peace.

1009) The world around me glows with beauty and magic.

1010) My heart is open and filled with love right now.

1011) All is well in my world; all is well everywhere.

1012) I love myself and everyone else unconditionally.

1013) I am becoming healthier and healthier every day.

1014) The energy of the universe flows through me now.

1015) Good things happen to me every day in every way.

1016) Every day, my faith grows stronger and stronger.

1017) My life is filled with love, joy and excitement.

1018) I am at peace with where I am in life right now.

1019) It is okay for women to wear whatever they want.

1020) I look for ways to use my imagination every day.

1021) Today, I welcome all the good that comes my way.

1022) My life is filled with abundance and prosperity.

1023) Life provides more than enough for me every day.

1024) I'm loved by many, who admire me for my talents.

1025) My body is the perfect weight for me, right now.

1026) My body is strong, powerful, and full of energy.

1027) My family loves and supports me unconditionally.

1028) I am always safe, even in unfamiliar situations.

1029) Life is taking care of me every step of the way.

1030) My relationship with myself brings me great joy.

1031) I am a source of love and a center of happiness.

1032) I practice self-forgiveness and self-correction.

1033) My whole life is blessed in many wonderful ways.

1034) It's okay if I don't eat perfectly all the time.

1035) All of my cells are healthy, happy and youthful.

1036) When I think, my thoughts are clear and concise.

1037) The more relaxed I become, the better I perform.

1038) My confidence and self-esteem are growing daily.

1039) People who truly appreciate me surround my life.

1040) I love myself very much, just the way that I am.

1041) I am a powerful, confident and successful woman.

1042) Nature blesses me with all good things every day.

1043) I thank nature every day for all of my blessings.

1044) I have the power to change my life at any moment.

1045) Breathing deeply brings me peace and tranquility.

1046) I am a powerful, confident and attractive person.

1047) I am exactly where I am supposed to be right now.

1048) Abundance is a state of mind, not a bank account.

1049) Money comes easily and effortlessly into my life.

1050) I love that I have plenty of time to help others.

1051) Every day, in some small way, I am growing wiser.

1052) I am filled with purpose as I begin this new day.

1053) My heart is full of love for everyone in my life.

1054) I easily release all of my resistance to change.

1055) I am open to receiving love and money in my life.

1056) Life is working out for me today very, very well.

1057) Life can be easy or difficult, it's up to me now.

1058) Today, I focus only on the beauty of this moment.

1059) Today, I show the world how beautiful I truly am.

1060) Love, love, and more love flows through me today.

1061) Money flows into my life easily and effortlessly.

1062) The world is a beautiful place filled with light.

1063) I am light, and I shine brightly everywhere I go.

1064) My inner child is safe, happy, playful, and free.

1065) All of the love in the Universe is within me now.

1066) I am safe and protected in every area of my life.

1067) All is well in my world; I am safe and protected.

1068) Everything that needs to be done is getting done.

1069) The universe supports me completely at all times.

1070) I choose to be happy, healthy and prosperous now.

1071) I am at peace with life's challenges and changes.

1072) Every day, in every way, I get better and better.

1073) I have a strong sense of self-love and self-care.

1074) Women work hard and deserve all the good in life.

1075) I am always in the right place at the right time.

1076) Everything in my life is so pleasurable and easy.

1077) My creativity is helping me achieve all my goals.

1078) Love, joy, and happiness are abundant in my life.

1079) The people important to me are healthy and happy.

1080) Peace and happiness are now flowing into my life.

1081) Whatever I focus on, I create more of in my life.

1082) Women are the most beautiful creations in nature.

1083) Today is a great day, filled with peace and love.

1084) My body is a temple, a place of power and energy.

1085) I focus on my strengths and accept my weaknesses.

1086) As a woman I have a deeper understanding of life.

1087) I will do whatever it takes to achieve my dreams.

1088) All of my dreams come true in every way possible.

1089) I have everything that I need to succeed in life.

1090) Today, I will be good to myself and my loved ones.

1091) My thoughts are healthy, uplifting and energizing.

1092) I breathe in positivity; I breathe out negativity.

1093) My life is filled with joy, peace, and happiness.

1094) My mind is free - it is open to new possibilities.

Affirmations 1095 - 1460

1095) Every day in some small way, I find joy in living.

1096) I feel great about myself and my life, right now.

1097) Everything in my life is working out for the best.

1098) The best choices bring the best results to me now.

1099) All that is mine comes to me, with ease and grace.

1100) It's okay for me to be exactly who I am right now.

1101) Every day brings something wonderful into my life.

1102) I am a magnet for positive, healthy relationships.

1103) I have more than enough love in my life right now.

1104) Abundance flows to me freely and easily right now.

1105) My inner child feels loved and nurtured right now.

1106) Everything I need comes to me with ease and grace.

1107) My giving attitude attracts tremendous abundance to me.

1108) I am one with life, and life is taking care of me.

1109) I trust that everything is working out in my life.

1110) My desires are being met in every area of my life.

1111) Nobody can push me around or influence me anymore.

1112) I send only love to everyone who has ever hurt me.

1113) I forgive myself completely for not being perfect.

1114) Today, I make a difference in someone else's life.

1115) My past only serves to make me wiser and stronger.

1116) My confidence is increasing with each passing day.

1117) Relationships are working out for my highest good.

1118) Today, I have lots of time for fun and relaxation.

1119) Everything is getting better and better every day.

1120) I give myself permission to let go and enjoy life.

1121) I am filled with gratitude for this wonderful day.

1122) I easily handle everything that comes to me today.

1123) I have all the love and support I need, right now.

1124) The more I listen to my body, the better it feels.

1125) My inner spirit is eternally beautiful and lovely.

1126) Today I rejoice in all of my past accomplishments.

1127) It's easy for me to be in touch with my intuition.

1128) I work hard towards achieving my dreams and goals.

1129) Breathing in positivity. Breathing out negativity.

1130) I am proving to myself every day that I can do this.

1131) Today, I will be positive, happy and light-hearted.

1132) This new day brings new possibilities and new hope.

1133) There is always a silver lining behind every cloud.

1134) I can do anything that I set my mind to and I will.

1135) I am striving towards my goals and dreams each day.

1136) I have plenty of time to get everything done today.

1137) I am surrounded by positive and encouraging people.

1138) There's magic in the air - and it flows through me.

1139) I am in the process of making my dreams come true.

1140) My thoughts are filled with positivity and clarity.

1141) My work today is deeply satisfying and fulfilling.

1142) All of my relationships are healthy and manageable.

1143) This pain is temporary, everything else is eternal.

1144) There is a perfect plan unfolding for me right now.

1145) It is my birthright to live a happy, abundant life.

1146) My mind is alive with creative ideas for my future.

1147) I love, accept, and forgive myself unconditionally.

1148) I am light, and the people around me are light too.

1149) Today, I am worthy of all the love in the universe.

1150) My success is inevitable; it's in the cards for me.

1151) My inner child is happy, joyous, playful, and free.

1152) I love myself unconditionally for exactly who I am.

1153) Every day I am more and more at peace with what is.

1154) Life loves me, and everything is going well for me.

1155) Everything that happens now is for my highest good.

1156) I am courageous on the outside, calm on the inside.

1157) Every day in every way, I get stronger and stronger.

1158) I take time to appreciate all the beauty around me.

1159) My body houses a soul which is divine and precious.

1160) My heart is filled with love for myself and others.

1161) I am a brilliant women filled with the joy of life.

1162) I have a clear sense of my own personal boundaries.

1163) My kids love me unconditionally, just the way I am.

1164) My kids have an amazing ability to succeed in life.

1165) Life brims over with opportunities to enjoy myself.

1166) I always have a cheerful attitude about everything.

1167) I enjoy the serenity of living in the here and now.

1168) My body is capable of more than I can even imagine.

1169) My immune system is really, really good at its job.

1170) Today I will accept the good that is all around me.

1171) My life is filled with possibility and opportunity.

1172) I am powerful because I have the ability to create.

1173) As a woman I am full of love for myself and others.

1174) People are attracted to my aura of positive energy.

1175) I will fight for my dreams even when it gets tough.

1176) My power is limitless; no one can hold me back now.

1177) I am good enough, no matter what other people think.

1178) There is beauty in everything, even the tough times.

1179) Each moment is filled with joy, peace and happiness.

1180) I feel good about myself and take pride in who I am.

1181) My mind is filled with positive, uplifting thoughts.

1182) I am powerful and free from worry about my finances.

1183) I love and accept myself exactly the way that I am.

1184) I am a magnet for good things to happen to me today.

1185) I release myself from the bonds of my past mistakes.

1186) I am brilliant, capable and talented - just as I am.

1187) Life always provides me with the best opportunities.

1188) Every day, I can feel more and more peace inside me.

1189) I am always in the right place, at the perfect time.

1190) My relationships are healthy, happy, and fulfilling.

1191) I am free; I am loved; I am powerful beyond measure.

1192) I'm doing the best that I can; everyone else is too.

1193) I can attain anything I desire; it is my birthright.

1194) It's safe to be me; it's safe to be who I really am.

1195) I release all fear and doubt from my mind and heart.

1196) I am at peace with the past; it's just a memory now.

1197) I give thanks that it is all working out for me now.

1198) Every area of my life is becoming better and better.

1199) Every day in every way, I grow into my greater self.

1200) Life is making it easy for me to take the next step.

1201) Today I have so much money coming in, it is amazing.

1202) I have everything that I need right now to be happy.

1203) Every part of me is beautiful and lovable right now.

1204) What a wonderful world it is when I get what I want.

1205) Natural abundance flows generously into my life now.

1206) Abundance flows into my experience effortlessly now.

1207) The most incredible opportunities are coming my way.

1208) All of my dreams are coming true in harmonious ways.

1209) I choose to see the good in everyone and everything.

1210) Abundance flows into my experience in many ways now.

1211) Creative ideas flow freely from my mind to the page.

1212) I am bursting with optimism and enthusiasm for life.

1213) I am bursting with enthusiasm and optimism for life.

1214) The more flexible I am, the easier change is for me.

1215) I achieve my goals by helping others achieve theirs.

1216) It is safe for me to realize my own value and worth.

1217) I am attracting loving and kind people into my life.

1218) What other women think of me is none of my business.

1219) Everything in my life works out for my highest good.

1220) I believe in myself and follow through with my goals.

1221) Life is beautiful, and I'm grateful for every moment.

1222) Today, I will shine my light and love into the world.

1223) I am surrounded by a loving and supportive community.

1224) I love and respect myself for who I am, just as I am.

1225) Life is full of surprises, and most of them are good.

1226) Each day, I do at least one thing that brings me joy.

1227) I release all past failures and regrets from my life.

1228) I am deeply grateful for everything good in my life.

1229) I love my life, exactly the way that it is right now.

1230) My life is filled with joy, happiness, and abundance.

1231) All that matters is right here in the present moment.

1232) I release all my anger and resentment towards others.

1233) I expect great things to happen in my life right now.

1234) I release my past and honor who I have become today.

1235) I never fail, because I am always being my best self.

1236) I am positive about all that is happening in my life.

1237) I am letting life take me where it wants to go today.

1238) Today everything feels so much better than yesterday.

1239) Life loves me, and so do all of the people around me.

1240) I am kind to myself; I forgive myself for everything.

1241) This is a new day, filled with endless possibilities.

1242) I release the past and allow life to move me forward.

1243) It's okay for my good to come into my experience now.

1244) I feel good no matter what happens today or tomorrow.

1245) I take full responsibility for my success or failure.

1246) The past has no power over me; I have left it behind.

1247) Today, I have so much money coming in, it is amazing.

1248) I am more in control of my life now than ever before.

1249) My mind is filled with peace, love and joy right now.

1250) The future is so bright; the path before me is clear.

1251) My life is a reflection of all of the good that I do.

1252) My inner beauty radiates through my outer appearance.

1253) Every day, I'm becoming freer and stronger than ever.

1254) I forgive myself for anything I have ever done wrong.

1255) I have the perfect set of skills to pursue my dreams.

1256) The world is a beautiful place filled with adventure.

1257) I am capable of achieving anything I want in my life.

1258) My determination is a strong point in my personality.

1259) I am now experiencing life from a higher perspective.

1260) My joy is contagious; everyone who knows me feels it.

1261) I am a woman who has everything she needs to succeed.

1262) I am happy and fulfilled in my current life situation.

1263) I am worthy of all good things that life has to offer.

1264) People love me just as I am, right here and right now.

1265) It's OK to make mistakes as long as I learn from them.

1266) Problems are temporary, but solutions last a lifetime.

1267) Every day, my intuition becomes stronger and stronger.

1268) I am selfless, kind, caring, compassionate and loving.

1269) I find joy in helping others and making others happy.

1270) I have everything that I need to be successful today.

1271) My life is filled with joy, happiness, and abundance.

1272) Today, I am open to receive inspiration and abundance.

1273) The power of the universe is working for me right now.

1274) I can achieve anything as long as I believe in myself.

1275) Awesome ideas are flowing in and through me right now.

1276) I am free to be me, no matter what anyone else thinks.

1277) Everything that happens to me benefits me in some way.

1278) My inner child is loved, nurtured, happy, and healthy.

1279) Everything I need comes to me now with ease and grace.

1280) I have plenty of time for everything in my life today.

1281) Healthy relationships support me; they don't drain me.

1282) My desires are moving toward me, and they always will.

1283) Life loves me unconditionally; this truth comforts me.

1284) I love myself unconditionally; this truth comforts me.

1285) Life loves me in a way that brings out the best in me.

1286) Life loves me for who I am; what more could I ask for?

1287) There is so much for me to be excited about right now.

1288) It's safe and fun for me to express myself creatively.

1289) There is plenty of time for me to accomplish my goals.

1290) My body is healthy, vital, strong, and full of energy.

1291) My life is full of fun adventures and new experiences.

1292) I create beauty and abundance in all areas of my life.

1293) I am a fun, playful person who loves laughter and joy.

1294) Every day of my life is filled with joy and happiness.

1295) My life is filled with joy, laughter, and spontaneity.

1296) All good things come easily to me in this very moment.

1297) I only attract loving, supportive people into my life.

1298) The flow of goodness into my life increases every day.

1299) My mind is in a state of peace and serenity right now.

1300) The day will soon come when I can say, "I've done it."

1301) It's easy to let go of things that no longer serve me.

1302) My attitude determines how well I deal with adversity.

1303) My creative abilities are expanding with each new day.

1304) In each new day, my creative abilities are increasing.

1305) I deserve to be loved by a partner who makes me happy.

1306) I am a strong woman and today I will be even stronger.

1307) My beauty will grow as my confidence and courage rise.

1308) My mind is always open to new ideas and possibilities.

1309) Every day in every way, I am becoming more attractive.

1310) I will find peace in the chaos that life throws my way.

1311) All my dreams are possible if I just believe in myself.

1312) Finding happiness starts with believing that it exists.

1313) There is always a way out of every difficult situation.

1314) The Universe has my back and is conspiring in my favor.

1315) The more kindness I show, the more kindness I get back.

1316) My heart beats with excitement as I start this new day.

1317) I am allowing myself to feel peaceful, joyous and free.

1318) The world always provides me with exactly what I need.

1319) Everything that happens to me is for my ultimate good.

1320) I am doing everything I can to let go of my guilt about

1321) Every day in every way - I'm getting better and better.

1322) I have everything within me to be happy and successful.

1323) People who lift me up and believe in me are everywhere.

1324) Each day gets easier and easier until it is effortless.

1325) I'm feeling more love for myself with each passing day.

1326) Everything in my life happens the way it's supposed to.

1327) All of the love in the Universe is within me right now.

1328) My life is overflowing with health, happiness, and joy.

1329) I am at peace with what was, what is, and what will be.

1330) Life loves me unconditionally, always has, always will.

1331) Life works out for me and my highest and greatest good.

1332) All of my dreams come true easily and effortlessly now.

1333) I have the power to choose what thoughts I think today.

1334) My intuition is giving me excellent guidance right now.

1335) It is okay for me to move on and live my best life now.

1336) Every day in every way, my body gets better and better.

1337) The more love I give away, the more love returns to me.

1338) Every cell in my body is strong, positive and balanced.

1339) My body is getting healthier and healthier, day by day.

1340) My body knows how to get lean and strong, effortlessly.

1341) Every day, my cells are getting healthier and stronger.

1342) My intuition is an invaluable guiding force in my life.

1343) The more I trust in the process, the easier things get.

1344) Every day is a new beginning where anything can happen.

1345) Today is a day filled with love, happiness and success.

1346) I have more than enough of everything I need right now.

1347) My creations are waiting to be manifested in our world.

1348) My creativity is increasing with every day that passes.

1349) Everything about me is unique and attractive to others.

1350) I am doing the best that I can, and that is good enough.

1351) Every day is a new opportunity for growth and happiness.

1352) I am deserving of all the good things life has to offer.

1353) It's okay to make mistakes as long as I learn from them.

1354) My mind is focused on achieving my most important goals.

1355) I am kind, compassionate, and loving towards all people.

1356) With every challenge that comes my way, I grow stronger.

1357) I release all fears and anxieties from my mind and body.

1358) I easily achieve whatever goals I set for myself today.

1359) My body is healthy, strong, vibrant, and full of energy.

1360) I am a beautiful and radiant being of light and energy.

1361) Every day in every way, my life gets better and better.

1362) Self-acceptance is the key to inner peace and happiness.

1363) Every day is an opportunity to create the best day ever.

1364) Every day, in every way - I'm getting better and better.

1365) Life has a beautiful plan for me, and I am following it.

1366) Today, I choose to focus on the beauty of all around me.

1367) I have all the money I need to achieve all of my dreams.

1368) The more I do what makes me happy, the happier I become.

1369) My heart is filled with joy; I am at peace; I love life.

1370) The world is a beautiful place; I see beauty everywhere.

1371) Healthy relationships are an important part of who I am.

1372) All is well; I trust that life is taking care of me now.

1373) Everything that happens to me now, I see as good for me.

1374) The more love I give away, the more love I have to give.

1375) Today, I choose to focus on all that is good in my life.

1376) Every day, in every way, I grow more and more confident.

1377) I am always guided to make the right choices for myself.

1378) It is okay for me to have all of this success right now.

1379) As a woman, I am smart, sexy and confident in every way.

1380) Life loves me and provides for me every step of the way.

1381) The universe provides for all of my needs, effortlessly.

1382) I see the best in others and lift them up with my words.

1383) The world admires me for the beautiful person that I am.

1384) I effortlessly manifest love and happiness into my life.

1385) My body has a wonderful way of naturally healing itself.

1386) Every part of my body helps me live a healthy lifestyle.

1387) The more I trust, the less fear I have about the future.

1388) An increase in my self-esteem is a great blessing to me.

1389) I am not responsible for other peoples' reactions to me.

1390) I am allowing myself to become more and more creative.

1391) All of life's riches come to me easily and effortlessly.

1392) I know it's okay to be me, and that makes me very happy.

1393) I am a woman who faced all difficult challenges and won.

1394) I can do anything; success and happiness are my destiny.

1395) Every experience in my life brings me happiness and joy.

1396) It's okay to take time for myself without feeling guilty.

1397) I will be fearless in pursuing my dreams and goals today.

1398) My life is becoming more fun and fulfilling all the time.

1399) The more giving I am, the more goodness comes back to me.

1400) I have plenty of time for myself living an abundant life.

1401) Money is just an energy, and it loves to flow through me.

1402) Every day brings new opportunities for growth and change.

1403) Today's affirmations are working their magic in my life.

1404) I have everything that I need within me to be successful.

1405) I am confident in my ability to make the right decisions.

1406) My life is filled with beautiful, positive changes today.

1407) I deserve the very best that life has to offer right now.

1408) I have enough time, money, and love in my life right now.

1409) Day by day, in every way, I am getting better and better.

1410) All of my desires are now manifesting quickly and easily.

1411) I am generous with my time, my money, and with all of me.

1412) Life loves me today as much as it ever has and ever will.

1413) I deserve love; I accept love; I am open to receive love.

1414) Every day in every way, all of my dreams are coming true.

1415) All of the love I've been searching for is within me now.

1416) The more love I give out, the more love comes back to me.

1417) This is a new year for me, filled with joyous adventures.

1418) My healthy relationships make me feel happy and complete.

1419) I am worthy of receiving the good that life has to offer.

1420) It's safe for me to allow life to flow through me easily.

1421) Every day, in every way, I am becoming better and better.

1422) I take responsibility for my thoughts, actions and words.

1423) Each day in every way, I grow more creative and abundant.

1424) I am capable of achieving anything that I put my mind to.

1425) I make the world a better place through my actions today.

1426) Each day in every way, I am becoming more and more happy.

1427) I love it when I catch a glance at my body in the mirror.

1428) Right now I am so happy, healthy and excited to be alive.

1429) I am at peace with who I am and what I'm doing right now.

1430) Right now all of my desires are manifesting into reality.

1431) Today I will focus only on things that ignite my passion.

1432) My heart is filled to overflowing with positive feelings.

1433) I am a natural leader who inspires others with my vision.

1434) With every breath I take, I am getting better and better.

1435) The more love I give away, the more love I have to enjoy.

1436) I have amazing ideas that help people all over the world.

1437) The more I love myself, the more love comes into my life.

1438) My heart is bursting with energy and enthusiasm for life.

1439) I am in control of my thoughts and feelings at all times.

1440) I know what it takes to be healthy, happy and successful.

1441) My skin radiates health and beauty from deep down inside.

1442) I am strong enough to make mistakes and still keep going.

1443) When I take time for myself, I have more to offer others.

1444) I am now willing to see things from a higher perspective.

1445) Today is a day full of positivity, success and happiness.

1446) My life is full of positivity, peace, love and happiness.

1447) I attract only happy, healthy relationships into my life.

1448) Life is unfolding perfectly for me, one moment at a time.

1449) I am a woman filled with creative ideas and inspirations.

1450) I am intelligent and capable of anything I put my mind to.

1451) Today, I will breathe deep and take it one step at a time.

1452) The more that I give, the more that life gives back to me.

1453) I trust that everything will work out for my highest good.

1454) I attract positive people and circumstances into my life.

1455) I have all that I need right now to be successful in life.

1456) I release all resistance to life, peace and joy right now.

1457) My path leads to the highest good - every step of the way.

1458) Life feels so amazing when I take it one. day. at. a time.

1459) Each day is a new beginning full of endless possibilities.

1460) I always have enough time for what's most important to me.

Affirmations 1461 - 1825

1461) My heart is open and filled with love and light right now.

1462) The more I love myself, the more love I see in this world.

1463) Everything that comes into my life serves my highest good.

1464) Today is the best day of my life; it keeps getting better.

1465) The more love I give out, the more love I have in my life.

1466) I am safe, and so is everyone else here with me right now.

1467) It's okay to be who I am because I AM loved and cared for.

1468) Every day in every way, I grow wittier and more intelligent.

1469) I have all that it takes to be happy, healthy and wealthy.

1470) Today is a glorious day; everything around me feels great.

1471) Every day, my conscious contact with source gets stronger.

1472) It is safe for me to release my past and trust the future.

1473) As a woman, I am filled with natural wisdom and knowledge.

1474) Everything in my day goes exactly the way I want it to go.

1475) I am a magnet for success and wealth every day of my life.

1476) I'm free to be me - lovingly, gently, peacefully, happily.

1477) Every day and in every way, I'm getting better and better.

1478) I accept all of the love that is coming to me from others.

1479) I remember that negative emotions come from false beliefs.

1480) The more relaxed I am, the better I perform at everything.

1481) Today I intend for my own works of art to come into being.

1482) Everything that I do is a work of art, and it's beautiful.

1483) Being a woman fills me with energy; it's fun and exciting.

1484) It's OK to hurt right now, because pain is part of healing.

1485) My potential is endless and I will accomplish great things.

1486) Today, I will be kind and compassionate to everyone I meet.

1487) Problems are only temporary, but solutions last a lifetime.

1488) My past does not define me; my future is what matters most.

1489) Everything is working out for my highest and greatest good.

1490) My work today will be efficient, effective, and satisfying.

1491) I don't need anyone else's approval for anything that I do.

1492) Life loves me, and so do those who come in contact with me.

1493) Having fun is worthwhile and brings happiness into my life.

1494) My body has the capacity to heal itself of almost anything.

1495) Today, I will dream of the best possible future for myself.

1496) I am completely brilliant, relaxed and energized right now.

1497) I give thanks every day for all the good things in my life.

1498) It is my divine right to focus on only the good in my life.

1499) Today, I will reach out and surround myself with greatness.

1500) Today, my thoughts are focused entirely on what feels good.

1501) I always attract wonderful, supportive people into my life.

1502) I am so excited to see what the rest of today has in store.

1503) Everything that happens to me today is for my highest good.

1504) I accept others as they are; I allow them to be themselves.

1505) Joy, happiness, and ease are now a regular part of my life.

1506) My inner child is learning, growing, and thriving each day.

1507) The world is filled with abundance and miracles everywhere.

1508) Today is a beautiful day, filled with love, light, and joy.

1509) I open to receive all of the abundance in the Universe now.

1510) I am so grateful that everything is working out for me now.

1511) Life loves me unconditionally, always has, and always will.

1512) Life is working out for me in positive and incredible ways.

1513) I can do anything; everything is easy for me to accomplish.

1514) All of the power in the universe is now flowing through me.

1515) As a woman, I always have time to do whatever I want today.

1516) Every day, every way, my life is getting better and better.

1517) I trust that everything is working out for my highest good.

1518) My body has the ability to give birth and nourish new life.

1519) My body is capable of healing itself, when it matters most.

1520) The more I give, the more that comes back to me multiplied.

1521) I am a woman who understands the power of beauty and grace.

1522) Today, I will act like the confident, free woman that I am.

1523) I like who I am and who I'm becoming in every way possible.

1524) Life is a journey, and I'm excited to see where it takes me.

1525) It's OK to make mistakes because tomorrow will be a new day.

1526) Every day is an opportunity to grow and learn something new.

1527) My body heals itself naturally without interference from me.

1528) I am capable of achieving anything that I put my heart into.

1529) Every day, I become stronger and healthier than ever before.

1530) The more love I show others, the more love comes back to me.

1531) Today is a glorious new adventure where anything can happen.

1532) It's okay if not everyone likes me - I'm cool with being ME.

1533) I am more than capable of achieving all of my goals, today.

1534) Everything that happens to me today is for my ultimate good.

1535) I am strong, powerful and confident in everything that I do.

1536) I love all aspects of myself - even the less desirable ones.

1537) Every day is a chance for me to start over and get it right.

1538) I have all that I need to be happy and successful right now.

1539) Today is an excellent day; it's even better than I expected.

1540) The world is full of endless opportunities for me right now.

1541) Everything in my life works out for my highest good--always.

1542) I am loved; I am lovable; and I am capable of loving others.

1543) The world around me is filled with love and light right now.

1544) It's okay to take care of me, and no one will ever get hurt.

1545) All is well in my world; I feel peaceful and calm right now.

1546) My mind is perfect. It is peaceful and calm all of the time.

1547) I radiate beauty, confidence and joy to all those around me.

1548) Things always work out for me . . . that's just how life is.

1549) Every experience is an opportunity for me to learn and grow.

1550) Each day in every way, my life is getting better and better.

1551) Each day, I see evidence of my success everywhere around me.

1552) I am so grateful for all of the wonderful things in my life.

1553) I am always led to whatever will bring me joy and happiness.

1554) I have the strength to follow through with all of my dreams.

1555) My life is getting better and better every day in every way.

1556) It's okay for me to be ambitious, powerful and hard working.

1557) My voice is always heard, respected, appreciated and valued.

1558) The more I focus on positivity, the lighter my life becomes.

1559) I am a powerful creator who is in control of my experiences.

1560) I am a magnet for love, success, happiness, and good health.

1561) I find it easy to be generous with myself and everyone else.

1562) Every day of my life is filled with joy, love, and laughter.

1563) I am making daily progress toward achieving all of my goals.

1564) Everything in this moment is exactly as it's supposed to be.

1565) The more time I spend in gratitude, the better my life gets.

1566) Being happy gives me the energy to do what needs to be done.

1567) Joy and Contentment are my companions every hour of the day.

1568) My joy increases daily as I release the judgments of others.

1569) I expect to win at all costs, regardless of the competition.

1570) Success is mine for the asking, all I have to do is take it.

1571) Today is a wonderful day, filled with so many possibilities.

1572) It is my birthright to use my creativity in everyday life.

1573) I'm thankful for my strengths and how they help me each day.

1574) I have unlimited energy reserves for manifesting my desires.

1575) Every day of my life brings me closer to where I want to be.

1576) I am a queen who deserves nothing but the best from herself.

1577) I am beautiful from the outside in, and from the inside out.

1578) All of my needs and desires are met effortlessly and easily.

1579) Each day, I am becoming a better person than I was yesterday.

1580) Life is precious and beautiful, and I'll make the most of it.

1581) Every day brings new opportunities for great accomplishments.

1582) I am allowing myself to receive all that I desire in my life.

1583) Money flows into my life easily, effortlessly and abundantly.

1584) Each day, more and more happiness finds its way into my life.

1585) Every moment is a new chance for living life to its fullest.

1586) I am a genuinely loving person, and people love me in return.

1587) I fully release the past, and live in the present moment now.

1588) Every day, I get closer to making all of my dreams come true.

1589) I am at peace with myself, the world, and everyone around me.

1590) I am safe, and everything is working out for my highest good.

1591) I am filled with love, gratitude, and appreciation right now.

1592) All is well in my world; I am safe and so is everyone I know.

1593) I have more than enough time for everything in my life today.

1594) Only good comes to me always; I trust that with all my heart.

1595) Today, all roads are leading me closer and closer to my good.

1596) I forgive everyone for everything I have ever been sad about.

1597) Every area of my life is filled with more and more happiness.

1598) Every part of my life is filled with more and more abundance.

1599) I am free of the past. Only good things are happening for me.

1600) Every day in every way, I grow more powerful and influential.

1601) Today is an excellent day; it's filled with fun and laughter.

1602) My mind is more focused, clear and positive than ever before.

1603) I am now lovable and worthy to the people that are around me.

1604) It is okay for me to be ambitious, powerful and hard working.

1605) It's okay for me to let go of people who are not good for me.

1606) I let go of my past now, freeing myself for something better.

1607) I choose my thoughts carefully, so they are always uplifting.

1608) My life is always filled with happiness, love, and abundance.

1609) I use my thoughts to create happiness and success in my life.

1610) I am a radiant being - filled with the power of the universe.

1611) Everything that I do is a reflection of who I am deep inside.

1612) Women were created to be beautiful, this is how I am created.

1613) Life loves me and showers me with abundance and great things.

1614) I am attracting more creative ideas to me, with each new day.

1615) Every day in every way, I'm becoming more and more beautiful.

1616) My confidence is growing stronger every moment by the minute.

1617) Every cell in my body is filled with light and magical power.

1618) I am a woman capable of doing anything that I set my mind to.

1619) I have the ability to help other people solve their problems.

1620) Every day, I am becoming a better person than I was yesterday.

1621) I have everything I need to be happy and successful right now.

1622) I am strong, capable and ready for anything that comes my way.

1623) If I'm feeling down, I will reach out to a friend for support.

1624) Every day, in every way, my life is getting better and better.

1625) My heart is full of love and compassion for myself and others.

1626) I am surrounded by loving people who accept and appreciate me.

1627) I am learning valuable lessons from every mistake that I make.

1628) With every passing day, my life is getting simpler and easier.

1629) I expect great things today, and I give it all that I've got.

1630) I have everything that I need within me now to be successful.

1631) My body knows how to heal itself, given the right environment.

1632) We are always moving towards our goals - it's called progress.

1633) I always have time for people who lift me up and help me grow.

1634) Everything in my life is exactly the way it is supposed to be.

1635) Today is the best it's ever been, and it will get even better.

1636) I love who I am; I totally approve of myself; I'm doing great.

1637) I am safe; everything is coming together in my life right now.

1638) Life is taking care of me now; it always has, and always will.

1639) Life loves me unconditionally; it always has, and always will.

1640) I am whole on my own, but I also choose healthy relationships.

1641) Life always takes care of me; it's a law that can't be broken.

1642) I give thanks that my good is being delivered to me right now.

1643) The world is a better place because of who I am and what I do.

1644) Today and every day, my life is filled with joy and happiness.

1645) As a woman I feel wonderful; everything around me feels great.

1646) Every day in every way, I am becoming more and more beautiful.

1647) It is okay for me to let go of people who are not good for me.

1648) It's okay for me to let go of people who don't treat me right.

1649) My inner beauty radiates to the surface and makes me gorgeous.

1650) I have an amazing sense of humor that makes others feel happy.

1651) I enjoy letting my mind wander and explore its full potential.

1652) My mind is sharp, clear, focused, and powerful beyond measure.

1653) I attract success and abundance with every thought and action.

1654) My hormones are balanced and in harmony with nature's rhythms.

1655) It's okay if I don't understand everything going on right now.

1656) It's always better to ask for forgiveness than for permission.

1657) I am called to express my love in the way that is best for me.

1658) Today I accept the fact that miracles are happening every day.

1659) Today, I am filled with love because today is a beautiful day.

1660) Today I am taking action to put my creative abilities to work.

1661) I give myself permission to be happy, successful and abundant.

1662) It's okay to be me. There's no need to impress others anymore.

1663) I am a woman who is capable of achieving anything that I want.

1664) The universe loves me unconditionally, just the way that I am.

1665) I am the type of woman who helps others in their time of need.

1666) I am a woman who lives with passion, purpose and self-respect.

1667) I am so grateful for all the love and joy I share with others.

1668) Love is the answer to every question I have or could ever have.

1669) Life is an adventure, and I'm excited to see what happens next.

1670) Every day is a new beginning filled with endless opportunities.

1671) I forgive myself for any mistakes that I have made in the past.

1672) Every day is a new beginning filled with endless possibilities.

1673) Money is just energy that I can put into action for my benefit.

1674) Life is easy and everything is working out for me every moment.

1675) I am open to new ideas, people, possibilities and experiences.

1676) My mind is full of positive thoughts that serve me well today.

1677) I give thanks for all that is working out in my life right now.

1678) The universe is conspiring to bring me my heart's desire today.

1679) I am learning to appreciate all the good things in my life now.

1680) I trust the power within me to bring about miracles in my life.

1681) I am worthy of receiving the best that life has to offer today.

1682) I love and forgive myself completely for everything in my past.

1683) I am so grateful for all of the blessings in my life right now.

1684) I am loved and loving; it's easy to love myself and others now.

1685) Life has my back. All of my needs are being met by life itself.

1686) My healthy relationships are growing stronger every single day.

1687) I am so grateful for everything life has to offer me right now.

1688) I have more than enough time for everything I have to do today.

1689) I forgive everyone for everything I have ever been angry about.

1690) Every single one of my cells is filled with unconditional love.

1691) I am grateful for the lessons that I learn through my mistakes.

1692) I am a source of inspiration and motivation to those around me.

1693) Every day in every way, my life is getting happier and happier.

1694) Every day in every way, I am becoming more and more successful.

1695) It's easy and enjoyable for me to take care of myself each day.

1696) The more I think about what makes me happy, the happier I feel.

1697) Abundance flows into my experience easily and effortlessly now.

1698) Every day in every way, my body becomes healthier and stronger.

1699) My mind is clear and focused with creative ideas for my future.

1700) Life is generous and gives me so much for which to be grateful.

1701) The love I have for myself shines through me as a radiant glow.

1702) I'm not responsible for how other people feel, think or behave.

1703) Today, I will act like the powerful, beautiful woman that I am.

1704) I can't control everything, but I can choose to be happy anyway.

1705) Life doesn't have to be hard; I can make it easy if I choose to.

1706) I have all the power I need inside me to create the life I want.

1707) The more love I show others, the more love I get back in return.

1708) My financial happiness is always growing more and more each day.

1709) I acknowledge all of the wonderful things I've done in my life.

1710) Every day is a chance to live my life to its fullest potential.

1711) Today, I will let go of behaviors that have been holding me back

1712) Every day is a new opportunity to change my life for the better.

1713) Today I will wander, explore, and listen to the world around me.

1714) Today and every day, I choose to see only beauty and positivity.

1715) Today is a wonderful day that only gets better as it goes along.

1716) The more I give, the more that life gives back to me abundantly.

1717) I create my reality; everything that happens to me is by choice.

1718) The Universe provides for me in perfect ways each and every day.

1719) I release the past and trust that life is taking care of me now.

1720) I deserve all good, and life loves me unconditionally right now.

1721) I am proud of how far I have come on my journey of self-healing.

1722) I have more than enough time to do everything that I want today.

1723) I am grateful to myself for always having faith in my decisions.

1724) I now release my past and set healthy boundaries for myself now.

1725) Women work hard and deserve all the good that life has to offer.

1726) Today I am so happy and grateful for everything good in my life.

1727) Everything in my life has perfect timing, for it is meant to be.

1728) I have the power to choose healthy, loving thoughts and actions.

1729) With each moment that passes, I trust the process more and more.

1730) I am determined to live a life that brings me joy and happiness.

1731) I am a lovable and capable person who deserves love and success.

1732) I radiate love and appreciation because it is part of my nature.

1733) Today I acknowledge all of the wonderful things I do for others.

1734) As a woman I am beautiful. As a woman I know how to love myself.

1735) The universe provides everything that I could ever need or want.

1736) I will not set limits on my dreams because of where I came from.

1737) I'm going to focus on the things that are going right in my life.

1738) Problems are temporary setbacks that will eventually be resolved.

1739) Each moment is a new beginning filled with endless possibilities.

1740) I am willing to see the world from a different perspective today.

1741) Every morning brings a new opportunity for success and happiness.

1742) I have the strength to accomplish anything that I put my mind to.

1743) I always have plenty of time to do everything that I want today.

1744) I find myself easily making time to do whatever I choose, today.

1745) My body knows how to heal itself when given the right conditions.

1746) Every day, in every way - life gets better and better for me now.

1747) Every breath I take brings positive change into my body and mind.

1748) Every day, I am more and more grateful for everything in my life.

1749) Today, I re-write my story; I choose to focus on beauty and love.

1750) I create my own reality with the thoughts that I choose to think.

1751) The Universe supports me now as I walk my path with joy and ease.

1752) It's my divine right to be always happy, healthy, and prosperous.

1753) It's safe for me to feel good about myself and my life right now.

1754) Deep within, I know the perfect timing of all life's experiences.

1755) The universe provides for all of my needs and desires abundantly.

1756) My success is inevitable; my path is (whatever the next step is).

1757) Today and every day, I do the impossible and achieve the amazing.

1758) I can do anything today; everything is easy for me to accomplish.

1759) I now attract people into my life who are trustworthy and honest.

1760) This physical form that I have been given is a miracle in itself.

1761) Today, no matter what happens, I choose to be happy and grateful.

1762) When I give cheerfully and accept gratefully, everybody benefits.

1763) No one has the power to make me feel inferior without my consent.

1764) Life loves me, and expresses its love through miracles every day.

1765) No matter what the situation, I know that my needs are being met.

1766) It's easy to take care of myself when I feel good about who I am.

1767) My smile is beautiful and it brings joy to everyone I meet today.

1768) Today is a day full of positive energy and endless opportunities.

1769) I am a wonderful woman who is brimming with positivity and light.

1770) Today will be filled with lots of fun and many wonderful moments.

1771) Every morning I wake up feeling refreshed and full of positivity.

1772) Through my work, I am able to enhance my own powers of creation.

1773) Every day, I am becoming the woman that I was always meant to be.

1774) Today is a new beginning where all of my dreams become a reality.

1775) Today, I will smile even if it feels like nothing is going right.

1776) I do not need anyone else's approval for the choices that I make.

1777) My enthusiasm helps other people look forward to what lies ahead.

1778) I am a magnet for all things positive and beautiful in the world.

1779) My intuition guides me towards success in all aspects of my life.

1780) I see the best in others and treat them with kindness and respect.

1781) Today, I will focus on the things that are going right in my life.

1782) My heart is filled with love and compassion for myself and others.

1783) I am a powerful creator and I can manifest anything that I desire.

1784) Every day, in every way, I'm getting better and better with money.

1785) I am open to new experiences and possibilities each and every day.

1786) My mind is filled with positive thoughts that serve me well today.

1787) My life has been filled with more than I could have ever imagined.

1788) Any mistakes are just opportunities for me to learn something new.

1789) I am worthy of receiving all the abundant gifts life has to offer.

1790) Today, I attract loving and supportive people into my life easily.

1791) Every day is better than the next; life just keeps getting better.

1792) Every day in every way, I am experiencing more and more abundance.

1793) The more love I give away, the more love comes back to me tenfold.

1794) I always have plenty of time for anything that is important to me.

1795) I love Nature and everything it is, without her we wouldn't exist.

1796) The world is a beautiful place filled with beauty and possibility.

1797) It feels good to take time out to relax and be still in the quiet.

1798) My body is a temple for my soul. It houses everything I am inside.

1799) Today I will embrace my inner-beauty and allow it to shine bright.

1800) My aura is glowing, shining bright and attracting positive energy.

1801) My business attracts amazing people who are supportive and loving.

1802) Every day in every way, I am becoming stronger and more confident.

1803) I am a wonderful, loving, and powerful person; I always have been.

1804) I deserve to relax and take time for myself without feeling guilty.

1805) I focus on living in the moment and feeling the excitement of life.

1806) Here and now, I am allowing myself to be happy, fulfilled and free.

1807) With love in my heart, I walk with confidence through each new day.

1808) Today, I own all of my power to create a joyful and fulfilling day.

1809) My mind is filled with positive thoughts that serve me well today.

1810) I am now ready to release all self-limiting thoughts from the past.

1811) I easily find the time to accomplish everything that I want today.

1812) I am unconditionally loved by the most important people in my life.

1813) It's okay to make mistakes - it's all part of the learning process.

1814) I am so happy and grateful for all the wonderful things in my life.

1815) Everything in my life is an opportunity for me to grow as a person.

1816) I only attract loving, kind and supportive people into my life now.

1817) Today I will be very successful as a woman in all of my endeavors.

1818) The more love I pour out to others, the more love comes back to me.

1819) My heart is filled with light; it shines upon everyone that I meet.

1820) My body is a perfect temple, it's healthy and nourished by my soul.

1821) I always have opportunities, even if they aren't obvious right now.

1822) Every day that I take care of myself, my future self will thank me.

1823) I will surround myself with people who are supportive of my dreams.

1824) With every day, I am growing wiser and becoming better at being me.

1825) I choose to feel happy and be my reason for feeling good right now.

Affirmations 1826 - 2190

1826) No matter what, I always give 100%, and no one expects more from me.

1827) Everything that happens is a part of the journey towards my destiny.

1828) Self-care is a priority for me and I take time for myself every day.

1829) I am now ready to release all self-sabotaging beliefs from the past.

1830) Today, I will share my gratitude with those who are important to me.

1831) Today, I am strong enough to take action on something uncomfortable.

1832) Everything works out in the end - better than I could have believed.

1833) Today, I will open myself up to new possibilities and opportunities.

1834) I am open and receptive to everything that life has to offer me now.

1835) The more positivity I feel, the more positive my experiences become.

1836) I am so happy and grateful for everything in my life - big or small.

1837) I release everything that no longer serves me; it's done--it's gone.

1838) The more kindness I show myself, the more kindness comes back to me.

1839) I am a magnet for all the pleasures and joys that life has to offer.

1840) Good comes into my experience right now, and it comes in many forms.

1841) I embrace my love today, and allow it to fill every cell in my body.

1842) Life is effortless for me; life loves me and supports me completely.

1843) I am letting go of my past now, freeing myself for something better.

1844) It's okay to let go of all of my problems - they're not mine anyway.

1845) People are very attracted to my vocal inflections and body language.

1846) This is a good day for me - It fills me with inspiration and energy.

1847) I am a powerful creator who creates beauty and abundance in my life.

1848) I am the master of my life; I live my life in the best way possible.

1849) Every breath is an opportunity to choose happiness & love right now.

1850) Every breath I take brings me one step closer to being my best self.

1851) As a woman, I am deserving of all the good things life has to offer.

1852) Every day, in every way, I am getting better and better at being me.

1853) Today, I will not give up and run away from challenges that face me.

1854) My life is a blessing from the universe; I live life to the fullest.

1855) My desire to feel good about myself is reflected in everything I do.

1856) I am a woman who loves herself, and makes choices that reflect that.

1857) I am at peace with myself, my surroundings, and the world around me.

1858) The more that I love myself, the more other people will love me too.

1859) I love being a woman, and celebrate all that it means to be a woman.

1860) I love to spend time alone, contemplating my own thoughts and ideas.

1861) My body is healthy, strong, and capable of wonderful things every day.

1862) Life is an amazing journey, and I'm excited to see where it takes me.

1863) I am capable of achieving anything that I put my heart and mind into.

1864) Life is an amazing journey and I am excited to see where it takes me.

1865) I love knowing that everything is working out for me in every moment.

1866) My life is a beautiful journey of self-discovery and personal growth.

1867) Life loves me, and shows me new ways to fulfill my desires every day.

1868) I am attracting love, joy, and prosperity into every area of my life.

1869) It is safe for me to express my true feelings, beliefs, and opinions.

1870) Today, I will maintain a positive attitude even when things go wrong.

1871) I am open to receive anything that is meant for me in life right now.

1872) My spiritual power and presence attract all good things into my life.

1873) No matter what happens in my life, I know that it is for my own good.

1874) Today, I allow the universe to bring the perfect people into my life.

1875) The world around me is full of love, light, and positivity right now.

1876) The more love I give away, the more love comes back to me multiplied.

1877) Today, love is all around me, emanating from everything and everyone.

1878) Thank you, thank you, thank you for everything that is coming my way.

1879) Everything is working out perfectly for my highest and greatest good.

1880) I have a radiant smile that makes people feel happy when they see me.

1881) All the love and joy that the Universe has to offer is now within me.

1882) The world reflects back to me the qualities I put out into the world.

1883) I let go of my past mistakes and experiences, without guilt or shame.

1884) I am the queen of my life. I rule over all that happens in my world.

1885) I am an intelligent woman who knows that positivity is my true power.

1886) I am grateful for all of the wonderful things that I have in my life.

1887) I perfectly accept my feminine sexuality as a gift from the universe.

1888) It is my birthright to help guide this process of creative expansion.

1889) I am becoming more aware of how to use creativity within my own life.

1890) The universe is conspiring with me, to help me grow in my creativity.

1891) I will become the greatest version of myself in every aspect of life.

1892) I am a woman who knows what she wants and is not afraid to go for it.

1893) Today, I will activate all of the power within me to achieve success.

1894) My hardships are growing pains that are pushing me towards greatness.

1895) The world loves me; I can feel it today. I radiate happiness and joy.

1896) Problems are only temporary setbacks that will eventually be resolved.

1897) Money is everywhere. It's just a matter of being open to receiving it.

1898) Life is easy and joyful. Everyone in my life reflects this back to me.

1899) My body responds quickly and efficiently to everything I ask it to do.

1900) Every moment holds an opportunity to turn my life in a new direction.

1901) I am now attracting all of the relationships that I have ever desired.

1902) I am happily taking daily steps towards achieving my dreams and goals.

1903) My inner child is celebrated, nurtured, and allowed to be playful now.

1904) It's okay to release the past; it has served its purpose for me today.

1905) I release the past and trust that life is taking care of me right now.

1906) Today, I move forward with my life toward (whatever the next step is).

1907) Every moment that I spend feeling guilty or afraid is a moment wasted.

1908) Soaring high above anything negative, I enjoy the beautiful day ahead.

1909) There is only one thing for me to do today; make it an incredible day.

1910) All of the love and joy I deserve comes to me easily and effortlessly.

1911) I have a beautiful laugh that reminds me to lighten up and enjoy life.

1912) I am a powerful creator, and I create beauty and abundance in my life.

1913) I am doing the best that I can. And so it is okay if it's not perfect.

1914) Confidence comes from knowing that I am always where I am meant to be.

1915) I have the strength to do what must be done, no matter how unpleasant.

1916) I have developed enough discipline to be able to drop negative habits.

1917) Life loves me so much, and shows its gratitude with so many blessings.

1918) Today, I will make an effort to remember how truly blessed my life is.

1919) Today is an exciting day, filled with lots of wonderful possibilities.

1920) Within me lies a wellspring of courage, self-love and self-acceptance.

1921) My creative abilities are growing more and more with each passing day.

1922) We all create our own lives with the choices we make every single day.

1923) Today, I will show up as an unstoppable force in everything that I do.

1924) I accept the way that life is right now, and feel grateful for it all.

1925) All of my relationships are based on love, respect, loyalty and trust.

1926) My thoughts are clear, easy to understand and full of positive energy.

1927) My potential is limitless, and today I will accomplish something great.

1928) I release the past with gratitude and open my heart to new possibility.

1929) I am surrounded by people who support me, encourage me, and inspire me.

1930) Every day in every way, my life is getting better and better right now.

1931) I have the power to change anything that doesn't make me happy anymore.

1932) Every day is a new opportunity to love myself more than the day before.

1933) Infinite abundance and opportunity are flooding into my life right now.

1934) I forgive everyone in my past, even if their actions were unforgivable.

1935) I am peaceful and at ease with everything that has ever happened to me.

1936) I give and receive love easily and fully, and it gets easier every day.

1937) As a woman I am healthy; every cell of my body feels healthy and happy.

1938) I always have more than enough time to do everything that I need today.

1939) I have a strong, loving relationship with my emotional guidance system.

1940) I am filled with enthusiasm for all of the positive changes in my life.

1941) I deserve to be healthy and balanced in all areas of my life right now.

1942) The more confidently I speak, the more positively people respond to me.

1943) Other people are drawn to me because they want to be a part of my life.

1944) My kids are amazing. They help bring peace, love, and joy into my life.

1945) Positive thoughts and actions build my confidence and belief in myself.

1946) I always have the power within me to be, do and have whatever I choose.

1947) It's easy for me to maintain my center and keep focused on what I want.

1948) Every moment is an opportunity for me to be happy if I choose it to be.

1949) I am a queen who deserves nothing but the best from everyone around me.

1950) I am a queen who deserves nothing but the best from life, and so it is.

1951) I am a brilliant and articulate woman who has a lot to offer the world.

1952) The Universe is conspiring in my favor and helping me achieve my dreams.

1953) My life is now becoming an expression of my true purpose for being here.

1954) I am willing to let life take its course with ease, grace and surrender.

1955) I am open to find the love, peace and joy that lives within each moment.

1956) Surrendering to the flow of life is the key to my happiness and success.

1957) I surround myself with people who make me smile and who lift my spirits.

1958) Today, I become aware of all the things that are going right in my life.

1959) I deserve to be loved just as much as every other person on this planet.

1960) Every day, I create my own reality with my thoughts, words, and actions.

1961) The best is yet to come; the best days of my life are still ahead of me.

1962) I release all resistance to love; love is now flowing freely through me.

1963) My inner child trusts that everything will work out for my highest good.

1964) I am one with all good, and it is flowing easily into my life right now.

1965) My heart overflows with gratitude for all that I am and all that I have.

1966) All of my relationships are based in love, respect and total acceptance.

1967) It is easy for me to keep my mind filled with positive, loving thoughts.

1968) No matter what happens, everything always works out for my highest good.

1969) People like spending time around me because they feel good when they do.

1970) Whenever life gets difficult, I find strength within myself to overcome.

1971) Today is a wonderful opportunity to create the future I want for myself.

1972) The more time I put into gratefulness, the better it gets all around me.

1973) Life gives me endless opportunities to be helpful, friendly, and loving.

1974) I absolutely love and adore myself. I am amazing in every possible way.

1975) My life is full of miracles; it would feel wrong to take it for granted.

1976) I will not let anyone or anything stop me from achieving my goals today.

1977) Today, I will focus on my goals and not the challenges that I am facing.

1978) My email and phone bring me only good news and messages of love and joy.

1979) The universe will provide for every need I have today, and so much more.

1980) I allow myself to be who I want to be, free from the opinions of others.

1981) A new and amazing life of prosperity, abundance and joy is mine to live.

1982) I'm a good person because I try my best to be kind and helpful to others.

1983) It's OK to make mistakes as long as I learn from them and grow from them.

1984) Today, I will focus on the good things that happen, and not the negative.

1985) I am so happy and grateful that money comes to me in many different ways.

1986) Life is very easy. All of my needs are already being met by the Universe.

1987) My success story has already been written; all I have to do is follow it.

1988) I am surrounded by angels who lovingly guide and support me all the time.

1989) Every day, I'm getting better and better at living in the present moment.

1990) My heart is open to receive the goodness that life has to offer me today.

1991) I am so grateful for everything that is working out in my life right now.

1992) It's safe to let go of the past; it is over and done with, and I am free.

1993) I forgive them for everything they have done that has hurt me in any way.

1994) I am compassionate toward others, and life shows me compassion in return.

1995) Every day in every way, I become more and more prosperous and successful.

1996) I am better than yesterday, wiser than yesterday, happier than yesterday.

1997) When I feel overwhelmed, I stop and remember who I am (and why I'm here).

1998) The more love that comes into my life, the more love I have to give away.

1999) My positive words have a strong influence over my mind and actions today.

2000) The path to joy is easier than ever before; it's opening up all the time.

2001) I forgive myself for past mistakes that made me feel insecure or ashamed.

2002) I am a beautiful and incredible woman who only attracts the best in life.

2003) The more I focus on the positive things in my life, the happier I become.

2004) Today is a day full of love and positivity, it's one of my favorite days.

2005) My heart is filled with joy; I will carry this happiness everywhere I go.

2006) I acknowledge my innate ability to survive anything that may come my way.

2007) I am the woman who is powerful enough to make all of my dreams come true.

2008) My life is filled with love, success and happiness in every possible way.

2009) Every day in every way, I am becoming more successful, healthy and happy.

2010) I trust myself, and know that whatever it is I seek is already within me.

2011) The best love, the best sex, the best relationships are coming to me now.

2012) Life is an adventure, and I'm ready to take on anything that comes my way.

2013) I can breathe freely, now that I'm free from negative thoughts and energy.

2014) I am thankful for all the healthy and supportive relationships in my life.

2015) There's nothing that I need to do today except be happy, healthy and free.

2016) I give myself permission to feel good about myself and my life right now.

2017) My past was necessary and important, for it has brought me to this moment.

2018) I am now ready to release all negative emotions from the past, one by one.

2019) There is enough time in the day for everything that I want to accomplish.

2020) Today, I will count my blessings instead of focusing on negative thoughts.

2021) Today, I am open-minded and able to see things from different perspectives

2022) I am not my thoughts; I am that which thinks my thoughts - pure awareness.

2023) Successful people do what unsuccessful people won't. So, I choose success.

2024) I'm doing everything right; everything is working out for my highest good.

2025) It's safe for me to have what I want, and it's safe for me to be who I am.

2026) Every cell in my body vibrates with the strength of my intention for love.

2027) The more loving and forgiving I become, the more love flows into my heart.

2028) It is safe for me to show others how beautiful I am on the inside and out.

2029) My intuition is an amazing gift that always guides me with perfect timing.

2030) All of my dreams manifest themselves easily and effortlessly into reality.

2031) I have all of the tools that I need to create a wonderful life for myself.

2032) The more positive thoughts I have about myself, the more my life improves.

2033) I have beautiful brown eyes that speak worlds to those who look into them.

2034) I attract positivity, happiness and success with every breath that I take.

2035) The world around me is beautiful, I will allow myself to feel this beauty.

2036) Today, I intend for my creativity to be showcased in everything that I do.

2037) I like what everyone likes and I like it that way. It feels perfect to me.

2038) I am loving, kind and compassionate towards myself and everyone around me.

2039) I am a queen; I deserve the best in life; it's all coming to me right now.

2040) The expression of my talents, skills and abilities is for the good of all.

2041) I see myself living a life filled with joy, happiness, peace and abundance.

2042) I give myself permission to forgive everyone in my life, especially myself.

2043) I give myself permission to be happy and live the life I always dreamed of.

2044) I forgive everyone for everything they have ever done to me or anyone else.

2045) I give thanks for all the good that is coming into my experience right now.

2046) My good is flowing into my experience, and it is safe for me to receive it.

2047) I am the most powerful person in the world, because I am taking action now.

2048) Today, I experience nothing but happiness, health, strength and prosperity.

2049) As a woman I am loving and caring; my energy is like the warmth of the sun.

2050) I celebrate all of my successes and triumphs with enthusiasm and gratitude.

2051) I am open to receiving all of the abundance that the universe has to offer.

2052) The more kindness I share with others, the more kindness I have for myself.

2053) Life is conspiring to bring me exactly what I need, at just the right time.

2054) My body is healthy, strong, and perfectly capable of taking care of itself.

2055) I'm making positive changes in my life by taking inspired action every day.

2056) I am perfect in my unique way; my body is healthy and nourished by my soul.

2057) I am capable of overcoming any obstacle because I hold the power within me.

2058) Today I realize that everyone around me has something positive to offer me.

2059) Today, I will be grateful for the little things in life that make me smile.

2060) I deserve all of the happiness in the world, and today I choose to have it.

2061) I am a woman who has the time and energy to do all of the things I want to.

2062) I am a woman who makes time for all of the things that are important to me.

2063) I am a woman who knows her own value, and projects that out into the world.

2064) Today, I forget about the past and focus on one thing.my current blessings.

2065) I'm a lot stronger than I give myself credit for. so why would I hold back?

2066) Life is full of beauty and meaning, and I will appreciate it more every day.

2067) Today will unfold perfectly according to the Divine plan of my Higher Self.

2068) Today, I will reach out to someone whom I have not spoken to in a long time.

2069) Every day in every way, I grow more lovable and loveable to those around me.

2070) I love who I am; the more that I love myself, the more other people love me.

2071) I am very successful; opportunities are coming to me easily and effectively.

2072) Today I will conduct myself as if everyone were looking at me and loving me.

2073) Every day my life becomes more joyful and abundant in all the things I love.

2074) I create beauty and love in my world every day with my thoughts and actions.

2075) I open my heart and allow all of the joy in the universe to flow through me.

2076) When it is all said and done, there will be no more me. It will all be love.

2077) Every choice I make is focused on bettering my life and the lives of others.

2078) I embrace my physical beauty, knowing it is a reflection of who I really am.

2079) Today, I will focus on the positive things that happen, and not the negative.

2080) My freedom is being happy and free from stress, worry or anxiety about money.

2081) I deserve to experience the magic of abundance in my life on a regular basis.

2082) What others say and do is a projection of their own reality, their own dream.

2083) Deep within me, there is a power that cannot be touched by pain or suffering.

2084) Today is a magical day that only brings opportunity after opportunity my way.

2085) I am calm, relaxed, and happy with who I am and where I am in life right now.

2086) All of my past mistakes are shining examples of what not to do in the future.

2087) I choose love, understanding, and forgiveness with everyone in my life today.

2088) I reinforce my own self-worth every day by living up to my highest potential.

2089) As a woman, I know that other people are attracted to me because of who I am.

2090) My positive thoughts help create a positive day for me and everyone else too.

2091) It's easy to focus on the good when you know there is only good in my future.

2092) I am confident, successful, and capable of achieving anything I want in life.

2093) The more gratitude that fills my heart, the more I will attract into my life.

2094) Everything about me is perfectly suited for success, happiness and greatness.

2095) Through the power of intention, I intend for my creativity to expand rapidly.

2096) Today, my talents will be put to good use by the universe who believes in me.

2097) Today, I will take time to be grateful for everything that I have in my life.

2098) Everything that happens to me takes me one step closer to achieving my goals.

2099) Every day that goes by brings me one step closer to achieving all of my dreams.

2100) It feels good to have more than enough time for the things that I enjoy doing.

2101) Each moment holds within it an opportunity to turn my life in a new direction.

2102) All of my dreams and goals are coming into form very quickly and very easily.

2103) I don't need to control anything or anyone in order to be happy and fulfilled.

2104) The more confident I become in myself; the more confident others become in me.

2105) Every day, in every way, I am growing more authentic, confident and empowered.

2106) There's no need to rush anything because this moment is going to last forever.

2107) The most beautiful flowers in the whole world grow right here inside my heart.

2108) There is nothing more to learn about this subject; I understand it completely.

2109) I release all anger, fear, worry, doubt and anxiety from the core of my being.

2110) My body is an instrument of pleasure and my mind is an instrument of strength.

2111) I have all that I need to be happy right now in this moment, and so much more.

2112) My mind is getting clearer every day; I am more creative now than ever before.

2113) I am a woman who has the ability to handle all of life's challenges with ease.

2114) I let go of all worries and trust the universe to handle everything in my life.

2115) I release any self-destructive thoughts and behaviors from my past immediately.

2116) I know deep down that everything in my life is working out for my highest good.

2117) My mind is filled with wonderful ideas on how to improve every area of my life.

2118) The more forgiving I am toward others; the more forgiving others are toward me.

2119) As a woman I am beautiful and radiant; I radiate love, peace, laughter and joy.

2120) As a woman I am feeling very happy; I feel the best that that I have ever felt.

2121) Life loves me and shows its love with so many blessings and miracles every day.

2122) I am a woman of distinction. I am a woman of excellence and great significance.

2123) Today I will share my light with others, it is all up to me to shine so bright.

2124) I am strong enough to do anything that's good for me, right now in this moment.

2125) I am more than what I have done; today I choose to be everything that I can be.

2126) The success of others does not make me envious; it encourages me to work harder.

2127) I deserve the best in life, and today I'm attracting more of it into my reality.

2128) I accept all of my feelings as they are; it's okay to feel what I'm feeling NOW.

2129) Everything I put out into the universe is received with gratitude and abundance.

2130) I am grateful for all of the wonderful things that are happening in my life now.

2131) I am doing everything that I can to improve my life, and I love myself for this.

2132) Here's another opportunity made possible through the power of positive thinking.

2133) There is always a way when I'm willing to put everything on the line for myself.

2134) It's hard to worry about anything today because life works out perfectly for me.

2135) I release my powerful manifesting abilities through love, joy, and thanksgiving.

2136) I take complete ownership for everything in my life - both the good and the bad.

2137) As a woman I am beautiful and perfect in my own way, I feel great about my body.

2138) I awaken in this new day with a new attitude, I am ready for all that it brings.

2139) I have the wisdom and knowledge to accomplish anything that I set my mind to do.

2140) Today I choose to be happy and excited for whatever the day has in store for me.

2141) I am a magnet for good people, good things and good opportunities in this world.

2142) My life is full of magic; I allow myself to be filled with wonder and amazement.

2143) It's OK to allow myself the time and space to feel good about how far I've come.

2144) I am feeling the wonderful sense of creative power, that is growing within me.

2145) I will never allow anyone to make me feel uncomfortable for being a proud woman.

2146) I am willing to be the best version of myself every day without fear or apology.

2147) Every day, I am getting stronger and more skilled at making my dreams come true.

2148) It's ok to let go of what no longer works in my life; it's safe for me to do so.

2149) I need very little space in order to create my life the way that I want it to be.

2150) I am strong, capable, and self-reliant - I can handle anything that comes my way.

2151) The world is abundant with unconditional love for me to share freely with others.

2152) As a woman, everyone admires me because of how wonderful and confident that I am.

2153) Today I will radiate love, peace, joy and happiness out into the world around me.

2154) Today, I will set aside time for reflection and focus on what matters most to me.

2155) I can achieve all my goals today if I work towards them with passion and purpose.

2156) I will not give up on my dreams no matter how many mistakes I make along the way.

2157) I am a radiant being of light and energy with the power to create my own reality.

2158) I am a wonderful, loving and powerful person; this is true in every way possible.

2159) I am a valuable asset to society, because of my unique set of positive qualities.

2160) If I'm not happy, I know I can find happiness simply by doing something different.

2161) Today, I will take care of myself by making time for the things that bring me joy.

2162) The power is within me to achieve anything that I want today, tomorrow and always.

2163) I don't need to change anything in my past, because I am a different person today.

2164) My inner dialogue contributes only to my highest good and the highest good of all.

2165) As a woman, every day I am manifesting lots of success and happiness into my life.

2166) Today my life is better than ever before because my future is bright and cheerful.

2167) I am so excited about life and the amazing opportunities that are in store for me.

2168) I can choose to change how I feel in any given moment by changing what I focus on.

2169) Today, I am going to take massive action on all of my goals and plans for success.

2170) I have all the love that I could ever need in my life right now, and so much more.

2171) Life is short. Today, I will take the time to do what makes me happy and fulfilled.

2172) Money is everywhere. I just need to keep myself open and receptive to receiving it.

2173) All of my past mistakes are lessons learned, and all future mistakes are prevented.

2174) All of the relationships in my life are based on honesty, trust, respect, and love.

2175) My inner child is unconditionally loved, nurtured, and supported by life right now.

2176) My mistakes are temporary setbacks which lead to rapid, even immediate improvement.

2177) The more I practice love and gratitude, the more love and abundance responds to me.

2178) My behavior is a product of my own decisions, not the influence of my surroundings.

2179) Today can be the best day of my entire life, it all starts with a positive mindset.

2180) Today, I will focus on the positive things in my life and block out the negativity.

2181) The more work I do towards achieving my goals, the faster my dreams will come true.

2182) No matter how bad my day has been, tomorrow is a new day where anything can happen.

2183) It fills me with joy to know that everything I do has a positive impact on my life.

2184) We are all connected. Money, prosperity and abundance are a part of everyone's life.

2185) Today, I will take a small step towards making a change I have been wanting to make.

2186) I release my resistance to life, and trust that everything is working out right now.

2187) Every day in every way, I am manifesting lots of success and happiness into my life.

2188) Here's yet another opportunity made possible through the power of positive thinking.

2189) The more joyous and happier I become, the more joyful and happy others become as well.

2190) My kids are excited about life; they don't get upset about things that don't matter.

Affirmations 2191 - 2366

2191) My power is within me and is always available to guide and protect me on my journey.

2192) If I can think of three things to be grateful for right now, my life will be better.

2193) The more positivity filling me up, the more joy I feel in every moment of every day.

2194) Every single day, in every way, I am becoming better and better than the day before.

2195) No person, place or condition can affect me emotionally for more than a few moments.

2196) I will allow myself to be filled with love today, for this is my most powerful gift.

2197) I will seek out opportunities to make my creations manifest, for this is my destiny.

2198) I deserve all the wonderful things that are coming into my life today and every day.

2199) I am letting go of my worries, fears, doubts and disbeliefs about who I am truly are.

2200) I am able to let go of my resistance, and trust the universe to bring me what I want.

2201) Today, I give thanks for all that I am, all that I have, and all that is yet to come.

2202) As a woman, everyone admires me; they all love how wonderful and confident that I am.

2203) There is a new standard of beauty for women today that requires them to be unhealthy.

2204) The more time I spend worrying, the less time I have to do anything truly productive.

2205) Good choices come easily to me now. Everything seems much simpler than it used to be.

2206) I deserve to be happy and filled with joy because I am a wonderful and caring person.

2207) I am worthy of receiving love from others because I am the wonderful woman that I am.

2208) The only thing holding me back is myself and my lack of belief in what I can achieve.

2209) I am confident that anything is possible if you work hard enough towards your dreams.

2210) Every day, I am becoming better than yesterday and no one can take that away from me.

2211) My life is full of happiness, joy, peace, bliss and unlimited abundance in every area.

2212) Today I will open myself up to receiving unlimited abundance in every area of my life.

2213) Every person on this planet is connected to me by a thread of infinite light and love.

2214) It's okay to release the past and trust that everything is working out in my life now.

2215) I release all hurt, shame, anger, blame and regret toward anyone who has ever hurt me.

2216) Every day in every way, I am letting go of my past and moving towards something great.

2217) I am a great communicator who always has new and exciting things to share with others.

2218) Being a woman is truly wonderful, I embrace my feminine side with love and tenderness.

2219) Today, I will be grateful for everything that life has to offer me even if it is hard.

2220) I will try and try and never give up no matter how many mistakes I make along the way.

2221) I am a woman of strength, power, and courage; I can do anything that I set my mind to.

2222) Today I will do what others won't so that tomorrow I can accomplish what others can't.

2223) My creativity flows effortlessly through me allowing me to express myself in many ways.

2224) My past is behind me, my future is in front of me, and all there is now is this moment.

2225) I am confident, self-assured, and capable of achieving any goal that I set for myself.

2226) I choose love over fear, joy over anger, gratitude over jealousy, and peace over worry.

2227) My thoughts are magnetically attracting goodness and prosperity into my life right now.

2228) I place my focus on what makes me happy and fulfilled, not on what others think or say.

2229) As a woman I am very successful; opportunities are coming to me easily and effectively.

2230) Life is taking care of everything I need - even better than I could imagine or request.

2231) Whenever a troubling thought comes into my mind, I will replace it with a positive one.

2232) Today I will not let worry, stress or anxiety get in the way of me achieving greatness.

2233) Today I will take time out of my busy schedule to relax and enjoy some peace and quiet.

2234) Today I will choose to see the good, even when I feel like everything is falling apart.

2235) Today is the best day of my entire life, I will not waste this opportunity to be happy.

2236) My life is full of happiness because I choose to love myself unconditionally every day.

2237) I have no fear of trying something new, trying something different or mixing things up.

2238) I have the most perfect body in the world. Every cell in my body is healthy and strong.

2239) My bills are all already paid, because the Universe is taking care of everything for me.

2240) What I focus on expands. So, I focus on what I want in my life not on what I don't want.

2241) My past is behind me, and today is the perfect day to create a better future for myself.

2242) Every single day is a new opportunity for me to change myself into who I want to become.

2243) As a woman, others are attracted to me because of how wonderful and confident that I am.

2244) As a woman, everyone admires me because they love how wonderful and confident that I am.

2245) Women have become conformed into an unnatural standard of beauty that promotes anorexia.

2246) The more positivity I put out into the world, the more positivity that comes back to me.

2247) Being a woman is truly an exciting thing because I am full of so many magical qualities.

2248) Everything in my life is working out perfectly right now and today will be no exception.

2249) Today my mindset is completely positive and focused on all the good things in the world.

2250) All the tools that I need to express myself creatively are available to me at all times.

2251) I will live my life in a positive way that is beneficial to me and the people around me.

2252) I am surrounded by loving, supportive people who are eager to help me achieve my dreams.

2253) All the patience, persistence and endurance that I need to succeed are already within me.

2254) The energy that flows through me fills my body and soul with beautiful colors and lights.

2255) I allow only the best things to come into my life now that I choose love and forgiveness.

2256) As a woman, others are always happy to assist me because they love how excited that I am.

2257) I am bigger than my difficulties, stronger than my problems and smarter than my mistakes.

2258) I have reached a level of wisdom where I can see others clearly without passing judgment.

2259) It's wonderful to be alive. My whole body helps me soak up this experience like a sponge.

2260) My intuition is always guiding me with love, wisdom, and clarity in everything that I do.

2261) I am strong and independent, even when it seems like everyone around me is falling apart.

2262) I have everything at my disposal necessary for me to live an abundant and successful life.

2263) Today I will let go of any worry, stress or anxiety that might have been stuck in my body.

2264) I release my resistance to life and trust that everything is working out for me right now.

2265) Everything I've ever wished for is coming my way - all I have to do now is think about it.

2266) My age is just a number, but my attitude makes all the difference in how long I will live.

2267) It's great to be the best that I can be and know that there's always room for improvement.

2268) My mind is filled with inspiring thoughts that motivate me to live my life to the fullest.

2269) I smile, laugh and rejoice on the inside whenever I see someone who is having difficulties.

2270) I claim my power over any stray thoughts that threaten to derail me from happiness and joy.

2271) I can do anything that I set my mind to. And today is the first day of the rest of my life.

2272) I am grateful for what I have, while focusing on the abundance of what is coming to me now.

2273) Thoughts once clouded are now clearing away like storm clouds in the sky after a soft rain.

2274) Every day I see women who are ill because of the belief that they are not beautiful enough.

2275) Today I'll walk to each person with confidence and say "Hello" as if I'm meeting the Queen.

2276) My power brings me all of the success, happiness and love that I desire in life, right now.

2277) I am now ready to fully let go of my past, and move forward in life empowered and inspired.

2278) Love flows through me, good things happen to me, and everything in my life goes well for me.

2279) All the difficult moments in life are opportunities to love more deeply and unconditionally.

2280) It's okay if you don't understand why I'm being passive or quiet right now, it's my process.

2281) Every day I have a chance to change my life for the better, and this is what I choose to do.

2282) The world is a wonderful place and every day offers amazing opportunities to learn and grow.

2283) My mind is open to new ideas that will help me shape my future the way that I want it to be.

2284) Abundance is not just about money. It's about enjoying life and being happy with what I have.

2285) Today, I give thanks for the changes in my life that make things better than they used to be.

2286) I am one with life, and it is taking care of me right now the way I want to be taken care of.

2287) Everything is working towards my favor; there's no doubt about it. So, what am I waiting for?

2288) As Abundance flows into my experience, the world becomes a better place for everyone as well.

2289) I create a happy and healthy home environment for myself and everyone else who lives with me.

2290) At whatever pace, I know that my body is learning and adapting to this new healthy lifestyle.

2291) I have the power within myself to become successful and do anything that I want with my life.

2292) I am a shining star in the universe that shines brightly in the hearts of everyone around me.

2293) I release the struggles of needing acceptance from people who are negative and mean spirited.

2294) Today, I will let go of my past mistakes, forgive myself and others, and move on with my life.

2295) The most valuable things in my life are not material, but loving and supportive relationships.

2296) Money comes into my life in many, many ways. I just need to get out of the way for it to flow.

2297) Every time I am feeling stressed, I release that stress and allow myself to feel happy instead.

2298) There's no need to worry now because nothing can stop me from making the right choices in life.

2299) Every moment presents an opportunity for me to choose peace and joy over stress and discontent.

2300) Today is a day full of joy, love and light. I am completely surrounded by beauty in all forms.

2301) I am a woman of great power and energy, who has the power to create anything I want in my life.

2302) My inner child is learning and growing every day as I teach her to love herself unconditionally.

2303) There's no way for anything negative to exist in this moment - nothing can escape my positivity.

2304) It is not in my perception anymore to consider only women who are thin as beautiful and womanly.

2305) My past is behind me. I embrace today with open arms and make new memories to be excited about.

2306) It feels so wonderful being alive and I will let this feeling sink into my mind and heart today.

2307) I have the power to manifest anything that I want in my life, through the creative force within.

2308) Today, I will not compare myself with others and I will focus on becoming better than yesterday.

2309) It's OK for me to let go of what isn't working in my life, and be open to new and better things.

2310) Every time I think a negative thought, I stop and think of at least one thing to be grateful for.

2311) The world needs me to be who I truly am so today I let my light shine bright for everyone to see.

2312) Life is too short for worrying about money. So today I'm going to let it go and just enjoy living.

2313) Yes, it's okay if I don't have enough time for myself today. I will make time for myself tomorrow.

2314) I feel the happiness and joy of my success, knowing that this feeling will remain with me forever.

2315) Why do things the hard way when life already has a proven track record of making dreams come true?

2316) There was never any reason for me to worry because everything I need already exists within myself.

2317) Every woman expresses beauty through their unique form, with their soft curves and sensual nature.

2318) Today, everything that I focus on becomes successful because my mind is full of positive thoughts.

2319) All of my needs are already being fulfilled by the Universe, so I deserve to have more than enough.

2320) Every day is a new beginning. So, starting now, I will look forward to what each new day brings me.

2321) I am conscious of every choice that I make and the effects those choices have on myself and others.

2322) My smile brings sunshine into the lives of those around me. My positivity brings joy and laughter.

2323) Today I will let go of my inhibitions and allow myself to live life to the fullest extent possible.

2324) I enjoy the wonderful things that life has to offer because my thoughts are filled with positivity.

2325) Every day is an opportunity to make today even better than yesterday and tomorrow better than today.

2326) It's okay if I look a mess today, because I'm doing what makes me happy and that makes me beautiful.

2327) When it comes to money, I trust myself first. I know that everything will work out perfectly for me.

2328) I am filled with gratitude for everything in my life right now; even things that may not be perfect.

2329) As a woman I have so much to offer the world in terms of love, passion, nurturing and companionship.

2330) I have so much to be grateful for in this moment because my life is filled with positivity and love.

2331) Every day, I am becoming more successful in every area of my life because of how hard I work for it.

2332) I radiate pure positive energy all the time, and this attracts wonderful people and situations to me.

2333) It is safe for me to be alive; it's safe everywhere in the Universe, always has been, always will be.

2334) Today is the day that I make new friends, meet new people and form amazing relationships with others.

2335) My life is now beginning to unfold before my eyes as joy and happiness come into my life in many ways.

2336) Successful people surround me now. They are everywhere I look. So, why shouldn't I be successful, too?

2337) I forgive everyone who has ever hurt me or made me feel bad in any way, even if they don't realize it.

2338) Every woman has beauty within themselves, they just need to express it naturally through their bodies.

2339) The more that I allow myself to feel good, the more that life will give me things to feel happy about.

2340) Today will be filled with positivity and I will make plenty of wonderful memories to be excited about.

2341) I am a woman of great power and inner strength, who is loved by everyone around me for all that she is.

2342) It's okay if I don't have a lot of money right now. What matters most is that I'm taking care of myself.

2343) I release the resistance to receiving my good, and allow it to flow easily into my experience right now.

2344) I deserve all of the greatest things life has to offer me - and through my belief, anything is possible.

2345) Today I choose to feel good about myself and focus on all the positive things about who I am as a woman.

2346) My life has great meaning and purpose. Every day brings with it a new chance to grow and become better.

2347) Everything about me is great, wonderful and filled with love. I deserve the best because I am the best.

2348) Today is a day to explore my creative side because there are so many wonderful things that I can create.

2349) The more loving and affectionate I am toward myself; the more loving and affectionate others are with me.

2350) My life is moving forward. So, should I - because if it's time to take action, then why would I hold back?

2351) Today is going to be a great day because every day that I'm alive I am becoming better and more positive.

2352) The world is filled with happiness and positivity, it's only up to me to bring these things into my life.

2353) My life is full of love, peace and joy; there are no limits on what I can be or have because I'm a woman.

2354) I am letting go of my past conditioning around money. Now, I am free to be happy and abundant all the time.

2355) I have plenty of time to play in my life. No matter what is happening around me, I always make time for me.

2356) I am proud to be a woman because we have so much power. We bring peace, love and happiness wherever we go.

2357) I am a bright light that illuminates those who are near me, today I will share my positivity with everyone.

2358) All of my needs are already being met in every way, so there is no reason to want or wish for anything more.

2359) My body is healthy and strong because my mind is filled with positive thoughts which support amazing health.

2360) Every day that I live is another chance at greatness. I use this chance to grow and learn more of who I am.

2361) My mind is filled with positive thoughts that are powerful and allow me to attract good things into my life.

2362) Every day of my life is filled with happiness, joy, love, success and all good things in every possible way.

2363) Today I feel grateful for all the love, peace and happiness in my life. There is so much to be grateful for.

2364) I have everything that I need in this moment and so much more because my inner-self is filled with positivity.

2365) My positivity is a gift to the world. I'm so grateful for this gift and it's time to share it with the world.

2366) Whenever I ask, the universe always delivers exactly what will bring me joy and happiness in my life right now.

Please Remember to Take Care of Yourself

*P*ositive Affirmations are a good way for you to start working on your development, but the quest for personal development is infinite. It is important to take care of yourself while you are developing. By taking care of yourself, you will be able to develop yourself better.

Taking care of yourself might involve eating healthy, exercising, giving yourself time to relax or even do absolutely nothing. You need to take care of yourself in order to be able to focus properly on your journey for personal development.

Personal development is something that can be done at any age. There is a saying that states "you can't teach an old dog new tricks", but this is not true. Adults as well as children can develop themselves and anyone can make Personal Development part of their lives, regardless of age. You should never feel bad or ashamed if you are still questioning things at your current age. The only way to know what you need in life is to continue seeking for your personal development.

Never give up on personal development. It is a worthwhile journey and the reward of reaching your goals is incredible! I hope this book helps you on your journey for personal development and you are able to become the best version of yourself.

The right time to start is now!

Feel free to contact me if you have any questions or suggestions. You can reach me at:

ViktoriaDavis@djts-publishing.com

We value your thoughts and opinions, and we are grateful if you took the time to leave a **review on Amazon. Thank you!**

Disclaimer / Imprint

Copyright © 2023 by DJTS Publishing

Made in the USA
Middletown, DE
25 January 2023

23074744R00066